The New Parent Survival Handbook

THE NEW PARENT SURVIVAL HANDBOOK

Sharon E. McKay

Macmillan of Canada
A Division of Canada Publishing Corporation
Toronto, Ontario, Canada

Note to the Reader

Any safety or first aid ideas, procedures, or suggestions in this book are not intended as a substitute for consulting with your physician. All matters regarding your child's health require professional medical supervision.

Canadian Cataloguing in Publication Data
McKay, Sharon E.
The new parent survival handbook

ISBN 0-7715-9228-0

1. Parenting. 2. Child rearing. I. Title.
HQ755.8.M24 1990 649'.1 C90-093054-3

1 2 3 4 5 WC 94 93 92 91 90

Design: David Shaw
Illustrations: Marilyn Mets

Macmillan of Canada
A Division of Canada Publishing Corporation
Toronto, Ontario, Canada

To Erika and Peter Redman,
who have trusted us with their friendship
and their beautiful children

Acknowledgments

I would like to thank the following people for their help in preparing this book:

Stephen McKay, my brother and copy editor
Philippa Campsie, Editor-in-Chief, Macmillan of Canada
Plum Johnson, Editor, Kids Toronto
Linda McKnight, Agent, MGA, Toronto

Chapters in this book were read by various professionals in different fields. My thanks to you all:

Julie Creighton, Past Chairman, Toy Testing Council. Currently Director, Canadian Marketing, Discovery Toys
Elaine Flett, Director, Tall Pines School, Brampton, Ontario
Virginia Mainprize, Freelance Editor, Toronto, Ontario
Ruth McCamus, R.N., Family Information Centre, Hospital for Sick Children, Toronto, Ontario
Carmen Paquin, Flight Attendant
Erika Redman, Parent Educator, Brampton, Ontario
Dr. Sonia Singh, St. Mary's Hospital, Montreal, Quebec

To the inspiration for this book, Sam and Joe.
And finally to the best reader of them all, David.

Contents

Introduction

It's no secret, I love my children. And in a world that reveres independence it may not be correct to say, "Anything happens to them, shoot me," but it is how I feel.

Why then could I cheerfully strangle the little darlings at any given time of the day?

Take my seven-year-old, for example. He's a bright, funny, all-around great kid. But why, oh tell me why, can he not put on his shoes in the morning? Here's a typical scenario. I yell (oops, I mean call) from the kitchen, "Are you all dressed and ready for school?" The answer inevitably is yes. "OK, get in the car." But wait. Child has no shoes on. "You told me you were dressed," I say while gazing at his shoeless feet. "Oh," says Child, "I thought I was."

Mind, we have come through that difficult period of right-foot-wrong-shoe. Rationally, one can say that there is a fifty/fifty chance of shoes ending up on the right (correct) feet. Nonsense. I have not yet met the child who can, even once, put the right foot in the right shoe. Then I hit upon a little tip. Place two discreet "X's" on the instep of each shoe. "When the X's kiss," I said to my shoeless child, "the shoes will be on the correct feet." It worked.

Take the dilemma of "mittening" an infant. Impossible you say, and up until I discovered this small tip, I would have agreed. I am not a fan of attaching mittens to a string and running it through an infant's snowsuit. It seems to me that string could too easily end up wrapped around his little neck. On the other hand, finding lost little mittens can take up the better part of a day. Ah, an idea! Take a child-size pair of tube socks, roll them over tiny hands and up their arms. The socks will not come off until I take them off, and the supply is endless!

Sensible, fun, simple, and sometimes silly tips are just what the situation calls for. It's true, parenting is serious and child rearing is tough stuff. And there are some topics, divorce, discipline and toilet training for example, that should not be reduced to tips. But sometimes, just occasionally mind, we don't need to know how to solve the Big Problems. We just have to get on with it without losing our minds (completely) and without, well, you know, strangling the little dears.

In a sentence, this book is for parents who have, even once, looked heavenward and said, "Thank you. I love them, really I do. But please, help me get through this day."

Sharon E. McKay

1

The New Baby

B.B. (Before Baby)

I don't want to scare you off here, but this period is probably the last bit of quiet time you will get for many months. Take advantage of it to rest, relax, and prepare.

Getting Ready

- Instead of sinking every last cent into baby's layette, think about what would make you a better parent. For example, instead of buying a change table (a potentially dangerous commodity), buy a telephone answering machine. Buy a dishwasher instead of a rocking chair.

- Buy a mattress cover for your own bed — unless of course you plan to replace the mattress within six months. Buy extra bedding as well. Babies leak. So do new moms.

I posted a 'Things To Do' Checklist on my bulletin board. To my delight my family and friends would come in and instead of saying "What can I do to help?" (which I invariably answered with "Oh, nothing!"), they would go to the board and pick a chore or errand. My dad came in and read 'Pay the phone bill.' Guess what he did then? It was wonderful.

Parent

- Buy a stack of paper plates if you don't have a dishwasher.
- Freeze small loaf cakes to serve the guests who appear to view the new baby.
- Arrange for a diaper service.

Do you want to get the rest of the family in the 'welcome baby' mood? Add half a cup of Ivory soap to the regular family wash to give all their clothes a faint new-baby smell. Don't overdo it — the intent is subliminal! Now don't be surprised to hear your skeptical seven-year-old admit that he too is looking forward to the new baby!

Parent

- If finances allow, hire a cleaning person for two days and give the house a once-over. Better yet, leave the house while all this is going on and have Dad or Granny supervise. If your

friends are getting together to buy a gift, why not suggest they pay for the cleaning service?
- If your baby is to attend day care, start calling around the day after you discover you are pregnant. Get on as many waiting lists as you can.
- Some new parents are so superstitious they won't even set up the bassinet before the baby arrives home. At the very least have enough baby stuff to care for baby during the first two weeks at home.

Morning Sickness

Morning sickness, especially the kind that lasts all day, plagues 60 percent of expectant moms. I fall into that category — with a thud! Most days I would get up, throw up, brush my teeth, and use a mouth rinse. Half an hour later the scenario would start all over again and repeat itself throughout the day.

Two months into my second pregnancy I ran out of toothpaste and mouthwash. I was forced to use my six-year-old's bubble-gum-flavored toothpaste and forgo the mouthwash entirely. Half an hour later I did not get sick! Hmmm.

After a few experiments with and without adult toothpaste and mouthwash I discovered that the toothpaste and mouthwash were aggravating an already awful situation.

If all-day morning sickness is your problem and you too have a "clean mouth'" compulsion, try this experiment out yourself.

The Buy-Buy Baby Checklist

General:
- Extra sheets and mattress cover
- Telephone in bedroom
- Diaper bag (an old beach bag will do)
- Several rolls of film (keep them in the fridge)
- Wrap-around dressing gown (to fit a shrinking body)
- Easy slip-on slippers
- Two large boxes of sanitary napkins

- Two to four packages of paper towels and a box of tissues for every room in the house

If you plan to nurse your baby yourself:

- Two nursing bras and pads (To make homemade nursing pads use a large-mouthed cup or glass and a pen to trace circles on a cloth diaper, cut out the circles, and stitch around the edges.)
- Two nightgowns (with slits or buttons down the front for easy nursing)
- Breast pump
- Emergency bottle and two or three types of nipples.
- A few tins of formula in case you get hit by a milk truck while jogging to lose that excess weight. (Also, call the La Leche League and ask for advice on how to freeze mother's milk.)

For Moms of bottle-fed babies:

- Bottle warmer for bedroom
- Four 4-oz bottles
- Seven to ten 8-oz bottles
- Nipples
- Sterilizer (unless you own a dishwasher)
- Glass bottles are best for infants; switch to plastic bottles when baby is starting to wield the bottle herself. Use plain bottles; bear- or bunny-shaped bottles with grooves inside will harbor gunk.

Bottles, and eventually baby food, do not need to be heated. In the first few weeks you may want to warm the bottles a little but gradually wind down to room temperature.

BABY CLOTHES AND SUCH

Resist all that advertising! It's a mistake to belly up to the baby counter and buy everything in sight. Buy the minimum. You'll be surprised how many outfits will be given to you after the baby is born. Anyway, you can always add to the collection later.

- Use an in-store layette shopping list as a guide only.

- Double the amount of stretchies and nighties suggested if you use a public laundromat.
- Buy a few infant sizes but concentrate on the nine-to twelve-month sizes.
- Avoid the three B's — bells, bows, and buttons. Babies sleep on their sides and then their tummies, so keep the frilly stuff on the front to a minimum.
- Pastel colors are fine but don't shun vibrant colors that will attract baby and put baby's pale (greenish) complexion in a better light.
- Zippers should not zip right up to the neck. Infants typically come with three or more chins and the lip of the zipper will inevitably poke one or two of them.

THE MINIMUM LAYETTE

- 5 undershirts (to be worn throughout the year except during hot spells)
- 7 to 14 stretchies with feet (may be worn day or night)
- 3 blanket sleepers
- 3 to 6 nightgowns
- 5 pairs of identical socks and/or booties
- 2 sweaters
- 2 daytime outfits
- 1 hat, sun or wool, depending on season (If allergies run in the family avoid wool and choose a synthetic material.)
- 2 bibs
- 1 one-piece snowsuit with feet or spring and fall bunting bag with feet, both to fit into an infant car seat

Note: Wash all clothes that directly touch baby (cloth diapers, undershirts) before using. Turn the feet of sleepers and stretchies inside out when washing. Threads and bits of fluff collect here and may wind around baby's toes.

LINEN

- 2 baby towels (Take a soft bath towel and one facecloth. Cut the facecloth on a diagonal. Sew the triangle onto the corner of the bath towel. Presto, a little bath towel with a hood!)

- 3 to 6 receiving blankets
- 2 blankets
- 1 comforter
- 1 set of bumper pads
- 2 to 4 fitted sheets
- 4 boxes of infant disposable diapers or a dozen cloth diapers plus liners and plastic pants

Even if you are planning to use cloth diapers, buy a small box of infant-size disposables. The birth may be difficult, stitches may keep you bed-bound — there are any number of events that may crop up. Prepare for them.

TOILETRIES
- Rubbing alcohol (to clean umbilical cord stump)
- Diaper wipes
- Baby soap and shampoo
- Thermometer (digital or rectal)
- Cream and ointment for diaper rash

Baby powder and oils are not recommended by many health professionals. If you do choose to use powder, however, try cornstarch. Put it in a large salt or cheese shaker.

Homework
Read everything you can get your hands on before baby is born. Once baby appears your attention span will be limited to reading the backs of cereal boxes.

Here are some books to try:

BOOKS FOR MOM

Pregnancy and Childbirth: The Complete Guide for a New Life, Tracy Hotchner, Avon Books.

Dr. Mom: A Guide to Baby and Child Care, Marianne Neifert, M.D., Signet Books.

How to Parent, Dr. Fitzhugh Dodson, Signet Books.

Children: The Challenge, Rudolf Dreikurs, M.D., Hawthorn.

A Sigh of Relief (First Aid for Parents), Martin I. Green, Bantam Books.
The New Child Safety Handbook, Sharon E. McKay, Macmillan of Canada.

Combing the bookstore in search of books that relate to your own lifestyle is a daunting task. If you can't afford a small warehouse of books, hit the library first. Then buy the books that you relate to. You will want to refer to them over and over again.

BOOKS FOR DAD

Papa need no longer feel left out. There's been an explosion in "fathering" books. Here are a few that are available in most bookstores. To order them by mail write to: Parentbooks, 201 Harbord Street, Toronto, Ontario M5S 1H6. Phone: (416) 537-8334.

The Father's Almanac, S. Adams Sullivan, Doubleday.
How to Father, Dr. Fitzhugh Dodson, Nash Publishing.
The Birth of a Father, Dr. Martin Greenburg, Avon Books.
The New Father Survival Guide, Larry Snydal and Carl Jones, Franklin Watts.
Becoming a Father, Dr. William Sears, La Leche League International.

Decorating the Nursery

Plan the nursery with your growing baby and finances in mind. Don't strive for some effect that your child will outgrow too soon. Easy does it. A baby's room should be stimulating but it's also a place to unwind. Do, but don't overdo.

Watch out for raging sexism when decorating. Pink is nice, so is blue, so are green and apricot and yellow. If money is tight (and with university looming in a mere seventeen years, it probably is), paint the room white and do your own decorating.

- Dip your hands in colored paint and paw-print the room. Use different colors. Invite grandparents, siblings, and neighbors to lend a hand. Have everyone sign his or her name under each print.
- Draw hundreds of happy faces with colored markers.
- Visit a wallpaper store and buy border or accent strips only. Match the main color in the strip with baby's quilt or curtains.
- Hang small baby quilts as pictures on the walls. (No doubt you will get several as baby gifts.)
- Decorate the room with various animal-shaped place mats.

FURNITURE AND ACCESSORIES

- A colorful shoe bag posted over the change table (but out of baby's reach) can hold all diaper-changing paraphernalia.
- If you don't mind the look of an egg carton or ice cube tray, use either to hold cotton balls, pins, and whatnot.
- Use queen-size pillow cases for sheets in the bassinet.
- Put up two paper towel racks within easy reach of the change table. Use one rack for paper towels and the second for rolled kitchen size garbage bags. Use the latter to take care of disposable diapers.
- Diaper pail deodorants cover up the smell. If you use disposable diapers, try lining the bottom of the garbage pail with dustless cat-box filler which will absorb the odor. (Put it under the garbage bag.)
- Replace the light switch with a dimmer. Or keep a flashlight handy for midnight checks.
- Table lamps are cute but take up space and attract children to a fixture that they cannot touch. Overhead lighting is better.
- Infants love to look at faces. Cut out pictures from magazines and post them on a bulletin board. Change the pictures often.
- Put a dust ruffle around the bottom of the crib and use the space as a storage area.

- Instead of spending money on crib sheets, buy colorful single sheets and fold them. The sheets can graduate to a single bed along with your child.
- Do you want everything to match? Buy four sets of matching sheets. Use one set to cover a baby duvet and make a crib ruffle, another set for the curtains, and use the third and fourth sets as bed sheets. Cover the rocking chair pillow with spare pillow cases.
- Layer the sheets in the crib. Cover the mattress with a sheet. Cover the sheet with a rubberized flannel pad. Add one more sheet. To change the bed in the middle of the night simply whip off one layer.
- Discard small area rugs or put rubber matting under them to prevent slipping.

The Birth

This is it. You can't change your mind, you can't go home and you can't go back. It will hurt but, to put it another way; a broken leg is painful. And when the leg is healed what do you get? Right, arthritis. Childbirth hurts but after it's all over what do you get? Exactly, a baby.

Preparing for the Hospital

Your hospital bag should include:

- Money for a taxi or parking
- Quarters for the telephone (and a few hidden bucks in case a fellow inmate escapes for a burger takeout)
- Insurance forms
- Preadmission forms
- Two lists of phone numbers (The master list should include the numbers of people to call as soon as the baby is born regardless of the hour, such as grandparents, aunts, and uncles; the second list, the names and numbers of people to call at a civilized hour. If this is a second baby, you may want

to write down the number of your firstborn's school and baby-sitter. Better yet, bring your whole address book.)

- Small bottle of champagne and plastic glasses (Label the bottle and ask that it be put in the fridge.)
- A very small bottle of sherry and small paper cups (The idea is not to lug around a mini-bar but it would be nice to offer a sip of sherry to a visitor who has come to see the new baby.)
- A pillow with two brightly colored pillow cases (Write your name directly on the pillow with a felt marker.)
- Nose drops (Despite the fact that you are in a hospital, the chances of it actually supplying you with little medicinal extras is almost nil.)
- A really nice housecoat that buttons up or wraps around and allows for easy nursing (But leave that gorgeous peignoir at home and mess up hospital nightgowns instead.)
- Warm socks for the labor room
- A stopwatch to time contractions
- Lip balm for dry lips
- Hard candies
- Pad and pen
- Camera
- Tape deck and headphones (Things do disappear in a hospital; if you decide to bring along a camera and tape deck, label them and be prepared to lose them.)
- Slip-on slippers that do not slip off
- Prescription glasses, blow drier or curling iron, sanitary napkins, toothbrush and paste, shampoo, makeup, and really expensive shower cream or soap
- Going-home outfit and nursing bra (You may arrive in your housecoat.)
- Baby clothes (undershirt, stretchies, hat, sweater, two diapers, blanket and, if necessary, bunting bag with feet)
- Favorite parenting book
- Birth announcements and thank-you notes
- Scarf or headband (You may not have the chance to wash your hair.)

And don't forget to put the car seat in the car for when you bring the baby home!

Pack for your partner:
- ASA or aspirin substitute
- Snacks: muffin, chocolate bar (which you will eat)
- Clean shirt, razor, and toothbrush
- Roll of quarters for coffee machine
- Box of bubble gum or chocolate cigars

We planned everything. My bag was packed, the car serviced and filled with gas. I had a separate baby bag ready. What could go wrong? We forgot to feed and water the dogs. It seems like a small thing but I worried about those dogs all the way to the hospital. My husband finally went all the way home to tend to them. My tip? Write down all the last-minute things that cannot be done ahead of time and post it on the fridge.

Parent

Post a "last-minute list" on the fridge door. You may want to:

- Feed the pets or call a neighbor to do it for you
- Turn on the answering machine
- Take a pillow from your bed
- Check the stove

You *will* forget the obvious!

Making the Adjustment: Mom
It's not uncommon to feel down after the birth of a baby. In fact the "three-day baby blues" (often beginning on the third day post-birth and ending around the seventh) occur in 50 to 80 per cent of new moms. But if the blues take you to new and

more dramatic depths of depression, or if you feel frightened of or antagonistic toward your baby, then you might have "true depression," which typically occurs from three months to one year post-birth. This depression is characterized by fatigue, feelings of despair and anxiety, loss of appetite, insomnia, or sadness. Talk to your doctor. She may suggest medication or give you a list of support organizations in your area. If that source does not work, call the local health clinic, resource center, or community library.

Small towns and rural communities are less likely to have established support groups but more likely to have neighborly care. Take advantage of your neighbors — the time will come to repay the favor.

I was afraid to go out on the balcony with my baby. I thought I might throw him over.

Everything was fine. I walked over to the stove to check on dinner. I opened the oven door, then slammed it shut and ran back into the living room. For a second there I thought I might put my baby in the oven!

Everywhere I go people keep saying, "You're so lucky," and "You must be so happy." Well, I am happy. So why can't I feel it?

New Mothers

- Bonding takes time. Falling in love with a baby from the moment of its birth is as common as falling in love with your spouse at first sight. Maternal feelings take time to develop.
- Your parents and in-laws might be horrified if you tell them that parenthood isn't all it's cracked up to be. Tell a friend who has children instead.

- Laugh. Rent videos of your favorite funny movies, read funny books, ban the newspaper or any reading material that depresses you. Just laugh.
- Have a beer.
- Eat all of your favorite food — don't go on a crash diet to lose that weight.
- Take your vitamins. Talk to your doctor about them.
- Exercise and rest, rest and exercise.
- Make lists of things to do and stick to them. Or make binding commitments.
- Plot out your days.
- Remember — this too will pass.

Your baby cannot judge you, read your mind, or become your image of the perfect baby. She depends on you, responds to you, and will reveal sides of yourself that you didn't know existed. But if you think that you may hurt her, put her in a safe place and get out. Stand on the balcony or front lawn, punch a pillow, slam a door, scream like hell. Get support.

There is nothing abnormal about postpartum depression. You are not alone and you are not crazy to feel this way.

Making the Adjustment

SIBLINGS

It is easier the second time around. Expectations are not as high and we all know what we are getting into. But don't forget, there's at least one little person at home who is entering a new stage of life.

WHILE YOU ARE PREGNANT

- Make a change in your child's life while you're still in your first trimester. Enroll her in a playgroup, get him involved in a new out-of-home activity.
- Let your child get used to "other-care-besides-mother-care." Employ a baby-sitter for short stints if you haven't

done so before. Get your child used to you not always being there.

- Take your child to one of your monthly prenatal checkups and let her listen to the baby's heartbeat.
- Go through your child's baby pictures. If you haven't done it by now make up a scrapbook for him.
- Cut pictures of babies out of magazines and together with your child make up a scrapbook.
- Avoid statements like "We will love you even when the new baby is born." The idea that you wouldn't always love him might never have crossed his mind.
- Lifting may be difficult but young children need to be hugged. Have special cuddling time in bed or on the sofa.
- Invite a baby over before your second is born. Your child will realize that she will not have a playmate right away and will have the chance to check the whole thing out.
- Take advantage of any in-hospital family services offered. Is there a sibling course?
- If allowed, and if appropriate, take your child on a prenatal tour. Remember to stop at the nursery window.
- Hit the library. There are a number of excellent books written for soon-to-be siblings. Read them to your child and talk about the upcoming event.

Older children may enjoy a more "scientific" approach to this baby business. Sheila Kitzinger's *Being Born*, photography by Lennart Nilsson (Viking), might fill the bill.

WHEN YOU GO INTO HOSPITAL

- Talk to your child about what will happen to him while you are in hospital.
- Let your child help pack your bag.
- If visits from your child are allowed (and if not, why not?), bring a few toys for her to play with. Small children are not adept at "visiting."

Before going into the hospital to have my second child, I packed my bag with a few treats for my five-year-old. When she came to visit her new baby sister, and after the cuddles and snuggles, I pulled out the treats. She behaved beautifully while all the relatives and friends cooed over the crib.

Parent

- Have Dad bring snapshots of you and the new baby home to your older child. (And wouldn't it be nice if there was a photo of your firstborn in the background!) Do not expect to see these snaps again. Your child might just vent his frustrations on them or take them to school and lose them.

We gave a box of chocolate cigars to our six-year-old. He took them to school and doled them out to all the children. His schoolmates were impressed and of course he basked in the attention.

Parent

- Send home hospital treats — bendable straws, packets of condiments.
- Telephone your child frequently but don't be offended if he "doesn't have time to talk." Most young children do not chat well on the telephone. Make the calls anyway but keep them very short. To keep the "Come-home-now-Mommy" tears to a minimum avoid calling at bedtime.
- Hide some treats at home and tell your child over the phone where to find them — one per day.
- Leave a picture of yourself with your child in his room.

Unbeknownst to my three-year-old daughter, my husband passed an infant-sized baby doll to the nurse. One nurse brought me our new baby while a second came in carrying the blanket-wrapped doll. My little girl was delighted to accept her "baby" while I cuddled our new son.

Parent

WHEN YOU BRING THE BABY HOME

Older children will regress to some degree with the birth of a sibling. Regression may take the form of a momentary pout or, depending on age and circumstance, your child may revert right back to infancy. A three-year-old, for example, may want a bottle, a four-year-old might demand to be carried everywhere. Be patient — this behavior will pass.

- When you come home, bring a gift from the baby to your older child. (Older children will see right through this. Use this suggestion with discretion.)
- Have a birthday party for the new baby. Your older child can blow out the candles and eat the cake.
- If your child is waiting at home, have Dad carry the new baby into the house. Your arms will be free to give hugs.
- Wrap a few presents for your child and hide them. When guests arrive with gifts for the new baby, pull one of these hidden treats out for your firstborn.
- Let your child unwrap the baby's gifts.
- Get your child involved with some of the care, such as holding the cream while you change baby.
- Avoid saying things like "He's just a baby, you are too big to cry," which suggests that you are siding with the baby.
- It may be a good idea to invite people over to see the new baby while your firstborn is at play school. (Visitors do tend

to get squeaky voices over little hands and feet. After a while, your older child will get sick of all the fuss.)

- There are days when your child will hate (not dislike) the new baby. Fair enough. Let her voice her opinions freely.

My six-year-old spoke in absolute terms about her new sister. When asked, she would say "I hate the new baby," or "I love the new baby." I realized that she didn't have the capacity for nuances. She just couldn't say "Sometimes I'm really happy about having a new sister and sometimes I'm not." I tried very hard to protect her from people who said things like "You should not say that you hate your new sister." I wanted to hear her feelings.

Parent

- Don't leave your firstborn alone with the baby until you know that she will not take out her aggressions on the baby. (Aggressive signs: a kiss becomes a bite, a hug a pinch, a pat a whack.)
- Babies can be annoying. Talk about them with humor.
- Laugh at the baby's antics together.
- Avoid calling the baby "the new baby." Give her a personality. Call her by her name instead.
- Babies cannot go to the movies, ride bikes, eat hotdogs, or do any fun stuff. Point out the advantages of being older.
- Older children may worry about added responsibility, particularly if someone tells them that they will have to care for the baby. "Who will care for me?" they may wonder. They may resent becoming part of the diaper-changing brigade.
- Place a stool by the crib so your older child may help with the baby care. Remove the stool if you fear that your toddler may use it to climb into the crib.

- *Safety Note*: Keep the crib mattress on the lowest setting to prevent your older child from trying to lift the baby out.

My son started to accept his new brother when we pointed out a few realities. He would be in high school when his brother was in Grade One. He would be driving a car before his brother had a speed bike. He would have a girlfriend before his brother was allowed to cross the street by himself.

Parent

- Your toddler may display his affection by dropping things into the crib for the baby. Use a cat net over the crib for protection at first, but you'll have to remove it when baby can push himself up.
- Leave the baby with the grandparents for a few hours and take your older child out on her own.
- Take your time fetching baby when guests arrive and let your firstborn have a moment in the sun.
- Your child may want to have a little holiday from school after the baby is born. He might be curious about just what goes on all day. Decide in advance on how long this school leave should be.
- Do not chastise or discipline your child while holding your infant. It may look like two against one.
- Don't go to the opposite extreme and forget to show the baby love in front of your child.

Useful, albeit well-used, quotes:
"You will always be older."
"I love you both, but I have loved you longer."
"In all the world, in all the planets, in all history there is only one you."

SPECIAL CONCERNS

Private Parts: It may be a shock for your little boy to discover that his new baby sister does not have a penis. Was it cut off? Does a similar fate await him? On the other hand, your little girl may be intrigued by this appendage attached to her new baby brother. Answer questions honestly: "Boys and men like Billy and Daddy have penises. Girls and women like you and me have vulvas. That's how we are made.'"

Nursing: Small children may also be curious about nursing. Can they have a sip? You may be uncomfortable about nursing an older child but chances are if you do, she will discover that "real" milk or orange juice is preferable to mother's milk. Express a tablespoon of milk for an older child who persists in having a sip. She will hate it!

PETS

- While you're still in hospital wrap your infant in a blanket for a few hours and then send it (blanket, not baby) home to the dog or cat. Let your animals get used to the baby's smell a day or so before you come home.
- Cats do not "suck air from an infant." They may, however, cuddle up to a little body. Place a cat net over the crib but be sure to remove it before baby can hoist herself up.
- Your dog may be an obedience-school star but past behavior is not necessarily indicative of how Fido will accept the new baby. Watch the dog carefully and train it to follow you out of the baby's room when you leave.
- Dogs are territorial and while they may seem to "protect" a baby who is playing in the yard, they are in fact protecting the yard itself. Using a dog to prevent child abduction is *not* a good idea. (Besides, dog doo-doo is edible — ask any two-year-old.)
- Large dogs may dash under bassinets, cribs, rockers, or high chairs and toss apparatus and occupant to kingdom come.
- Use a child safety gate to keep pets out of the nursery.

2

Life with Baby

Crying

All babies cry, some as much as two to four hours a day by the time they are six weeks old or so. The cries do taper off by twelve weeks or so.

Babies cry because they are lonely, fussy, in pain, sick, itchy, cold, hot, want to change position, have gas, need a diaper change, want to make their presence known or want to block out the world. They may be mad, hungry, bored, colicky, frustrated — or they cry because they just plain feel like it. Whatever the reason (and all these reasons are valid) they have the right to be heard and responded to.

If you are concerned, talk to your child's doctor.

Quelling the waters:

- Stick a blanket in the dryer for a few minutes, wrap baby in it, and hold her close.
- Take a bath with her.
- Remove her clothes and let her kick freely.
- Check clothing to see that it is not binding.
- Bundle her up in fetal fashion.
- Introduce a pacifier by warming it slightly in water and gently holding it in baby's mouth until she gets the hang of sucking on it.
- Try using a mechanical swing.
- Give baby a massage (read *The Complete Book of Massage*, Clare Maxwell Hudson, Macmillan).
- If baby cries every day between four and five and is comforted by a stroll in the park, for example, then plan your afternoon accordingly.
- There is emerging evidence to suggest that a device (similar to a massage machine) attached to the bed will gently shake baby to sleep. A ride in a car might produce the same effect.
- Try putting a hot water bottle (but make it lukewarm) on baby's tummy. *Do not*, however, let baby sleep on a heating pad. If you want to warm the cot with a pad, do so, but remove the pad before putting baby to bed.

It got to the point where my husband would walk in the door at night with his arms outstretched just in case I pitched our ever-tearful baby at him. I tried every trick I could think of to stop our baby from crying. One evening my husband came home, undressed down to his shorts, lay down, and draped the baby over his stomach. Our baby immediately stopped crying. With our baby peacefully snoozing away on his tummy, my husband read the paper.

Parent

The "C" Word

There is still considerable debate as to whether colic actually exists or not. Nuts. Colic does exist (ask any parent who has been there). If you have a colicky baby and your child's doctor does not believe colic "exists", change doctors. But do not diagnose colic yourself. Only your child's doctor can rule out other causes such as ear, nose, throat, urinary, or gastric infections.

A baby with colic is typically between one and three months old. Statistics suggest that 20 percent of all babies are colicky to some degree. Colic often rears its ugly head after a feeding or in the early evening. In some cases it lasts all day and all night.

Baby is in pain. He may also be constipated, or constipation may follow a bout with colic. His cries seem different from "normal" crying. But what really is colic and what is its cause? No one knows for sure, so best get on with surviving it.

- To eliminate gas bring baby's knees up to his chest.
- Review your diet if you are nursing. Some mothers have reported that garlic, caffeine, chocolate, oysters, and wine bring on their baby's tears.
- If you are bottle-feeding your baby, consider switching formulas.

I couldn't believe that a baby could cry this much. I took her to two doctors. Both said she was fine and one suggested that I get help. I took her to a third doctor who discovered that she had a painful inner ear infection.

Parent

It's not your fault. You are not a bad mother nor is your baby spoiled. Some babies develop colic, others don't. Some babies are difficult, some are not. Remember, this will pass. Until then take care of *yourself* by:

- Getting your hair done. Having a facial.
- Taking a hot bath.
- Calling a baby-sitter.
- Standing on your front porch and contemplating the daisies.
- Pounding a pillow.
- Listening to music — hard rock may be preferred by your infant.
- Getting support.
- Having a good cry.

It's hard. It's bad enough that a new parent must cope with hemorrhoids, lack of sleep, and often financial difficulty. The addition of colic may seem as if your baby has declared war.

Resentment toward a baby is normal — after all, being hollered at several hours a day would make the best of us testy. If that resentment takes on a violent twist, however, *get help fast.* Call a "hot" (emergency) or "warm" (support) telephone line. Your local health unit or nurse may help you get in touch with another parent in the same situation or may suggest a support group. Ask for all the help you can get.

Sleep

In case no one has told you, babies only sleep when you have to be up. Still, here are some ways to hasten the arrival of the Sandman.

- Make sure that baby has enough daytime activity.
- Get baby used to "sleepy-time music" Sing a special song or play a special tape to signify bedtime.
- Give your baby a massage.

- If you use a specific brand of perfume, dab a little on the baby's blankets. (Babies have been known to react to a change in smells. If you switch perfumes, watch your baby's reaction.)
- Change diapers before nursing baby. Once baby has fallen asleep don't wake her up to change her diaper.
- Warm the sheets with a hot water bottle or heating pad. *Always* remove the pad before putting baby to bed.
- Swaddle baby in the fetal position.
- Check the bedroom for too many distractions. A crib that has several mobiles over it, for example, can be too distracting for a little fellow.
- Some babies do not want to be swaddled; they prefer to kick freely.
- Do not cover little hands with mitts. Fists are tasty.

And when you get desperate:

- Take a midnight stroll with baby.
- Put baby in a car seat and go for a drive.
- The washing machine or dryer can sometimes lull a baby into sleep. Put her in a baby seat and place baby plus seat on top of the machine but note — the vibrations could move the seat to the edge so *never, ever leave her alone.*

When I was a kid my mother always insisted on complete silence when "the baby" (one of my siblings) was napping. Since there always seemed to be a baby in the house I grew up in a morgue-like atmosphere. I began to resent my siblings for the imposed silence. We are now all very light sleepers. My three kids are not cocooned in silence when they nap and as a result they can sleep through anything. I have even vacuumed during their naps.

Parent

- Turn on a fan (low setting) and direct it away from baby. "White" noise can be soothing.
- Snuggle baby up by pressing her back against the crib's bumper pads with her head lightly brushing the top of the crib. Bunch or tuck a small blanket near her tummy. This fetal position can be soothing. (Never use pillows, which could cause suffocation.)
- Puppies like it, babies may too! Put a loud ticking clock in the nursery.

Safety Note: You've heard it before. For the sake of her teeth, do not let baby fall asleep with a milk- or juice-filled bottle. Choking and ear infections are other possible side effects of a baby or toddler falling asleep with a bottle.

Rocking or singing a baby to sleep can be wonderfully soothing for baby and parent, but in the long run it's best if baby gets used to falling asleep in his cot or crib. The message should be "This is my bed, beds are for sleeping"

To give baby that extra security in the crib while nursing or cuddling, rub an exposed arm or leg with a soft blanket or stuffed toy. Put the blanket or toy in the crib with baby. (Choose a security blanket or toy with care — it may be around for a long time. It should be completely washable, very durable, and any color but white.)

Bathing Baby

There are two objectives to bathing a baby. Only one is to get her clean. Getting a child used to water is also important, which means bath time should be fun for both of you.

Bath Time

- Daily baths are not always necessary, although daily sponging of face, neck, hands and bum is important.
- Since you can never, ever, leave a baby or young child alone in the bath, collect all bathing paraphernalia in advance —

towel, facecloth, soap, cotton balls, creams, diaper, clean clothes.
- Take the phone off the hook or switch on the answering machine.
- Try not to bath a baby just before or just after she eats.
- Wash baby with a cloth very gently. Remember to play, sing, and laugh as you go.
- Soap designed for adults is rarely necessary and never use it on baby's face.
- Liquid soap in a pump bottle can be put directly into the bath. The water will warm it up.
- Shampoo baby twice a week unless there is a problem with cradle cap.
- A dab of petroleum jelly over each eyebrow may keep soapy water or shampoo from dribbling into baby's eyes.

More liquid vitamins dribble down my child's front than seem to go into her mouth. And have you ever noticed that all liquid medicines seem to stain? What is it — a plot? The best place to give a young child vitamins or medicines is in the tub. (Just make sure that in the event of a struggle your child doesn't slip under the water!)

Parent

- Clean eyes with dampened cotton balls — one ball per eye.
- "Blow-up" or inflatable portable baths are handy but bath-water may cool quickly. If the portable bath is placed in an adult tub and surrounded by warm water, the temperature will stay consistent.
- If you use the kitchen sink as a tub, turn the hot water off before you turn off the cold. The last bit of water to flow

through the faucet will then be cold water, which will cool off the faucet.

- Use clothes pegs to pin a towel against you — bib fashion. The towel will keep you more or less dry and can be wrapped around baby quickly.
- A small towel placed in the bottom of the tub and covered with water will prevent baby from slipping around. To prop him up, keep one hand under his neck.
- About uncircumcised penises: Hands off! Do not try and retract the foreskin. Nature has its own way of keeping the penis clean. If you have any concerns, take them to your child's doctor.
- During the interim stage in which your child is a bit too old for an infant tub but not yet ready for the family bathtub, put a soft plastic laundry basket in the tub. A child between twelve months and two years will grab hold of the sides and play. Careful though — your child could tip the whole contraption over without your constant surveillance.
- Do you need to use baby powder? If you must, prevent baby from inhaling the powder by first pouring it into your cupped hand and then sprinkling it on baby. Since many baby powders come in milk bottle shapes, put it out of reach or baby might try and gulp it down.

Bathing with Baby

Do not enter the tub holding onto a baby. Place baby and towel in an infant seat (perhaps a car seat) on the bathroom floor. Get into the tub and sit down. Now reach over and pull baby into the bath with you. When it's time to get out, put baby back into the seat and wrap the towel around him. Now slide back under the water and enjoy a few moments on your own.

Nail Care

An infant may need her nails cut to prevent her from scratching her face. Use baby nail scissors or clippers with rounded tips. Clip the nails when baby is asleep or have someone else do it when she is nursing.

Food for Baby (and the Floor, the Walls, the Dog . . .)

Bottle-Feeding

Breast is best, of course, but there may be many reasons why it is not right for you. The following is a list of tips for parents who are bottle-feeding.

- Wash the tops of formula cans before opening. Also wash your can opener regularly. Can openers collect goop in the movable parts.
- Keep opened cans of formula covered. Watch the expiration dates. Read label for storing instructions.
- Remember, formula separates when frozen.
- Electric baby-bottle warmers are great in the bedroom for those early morning feeds, but if you don't have one, put a bottle in a wide-mouthed thermos and fill with boiling water. Depending on when the bottle is needed, the milk should keep warm.
- To break baby's suction when bottle-feeding, or nursing, put your finger in the corner of baby's mouth.
- Use day-old formula as a base for sauces or cream soups or give it to your pet.
- Change baby's diapers before feeding time in case she drifts off.
- Enlarge nipple holes by poking a hot needle through the middle. Toss out nipples in which the holes are too big.
- Examine nipples for tears and rips by holding them up to the light.
- To sterilize baby-bottle nipples in a microwave, add a teaspoon of vinegar to a jar filled with water, pop in the nipples, and mike on high.
- Baby-bottle nipples will scatter in your dishwasher and possibly damage the interior. Put them in a mesh bag.

- Choose see-through baby bottles, preferably ones without grooves on the inside. The more twists and turns, the harder it is to clean properly.
- Get rid of the sour milky smell in the bottle by filling it with a teaspoon of baking soda and warm water. Let stand overnight.
- Use cardboard soft-drink cartons to store bottles in the fridge.
- Serve baby juice at room temperature. Juice tends to lose vitamins when heated and if baby is used to room temperature or even cool juice, you'll eliminate that heating problem when out and about.

LA LECHE LEAGUE (LLL)

An international, non-profit organization which provides support and information to women who choose to breast-feed their babies. In Canada: LLL Canadian Office, 493 Main St., Winchester, Ontario. K0C 2K0 (613) 774-2850. In the U.S.A.: LLL International, P.0. Box 1209, Franklin Park, IL., 60131-8209 U.S.A. (708) 455-7730.

Weaning

Breast-fed babies should be introduced to a bottle as soon as they are well established on the breast (1 to 3 months). Here are steps to introduce a breast-fed baby to a bottle:

- Choose a large nipple. The Playtex "Natural Action" Infant Baby nipple works well but you may have to experiment. Warm it under warm water.
- Keep the taste familiar. Fill the bottle with warmed mother's milk.
- Jam the warmed bottle nipple right into baby's face and don't be polite about it. This sounds odd, so let me explain. When a breast-fed baby nurses, he is pressed right up against the breast. He feels mom's skin against his cheeks, nose, and skin. Obviously baby has to breathe, but the idea is to simulate that same feeling.

- Have someone else feed baby. Baby may refuse the bottle if he knows the real thing is inches away.
- If you plan to nurse in the evening and have baby bottle-fed during the day (i.e. you plan to return to work), gradually mix formula in with the mother's milk. Your own body will adjust the milk flow accordingly.
- There have been no zillion-dollar studies to prove this point, but it stands to reason that a baby who sucks on a pacifier (dummy) will more readily accept the nipple of a bottle.

Weaning a child from the bottle can be a snap (if the child directs the proceedings) or bloody awful (if a parent runs the show). Before you even attempt it, ask yourself if it's mother-in-law or you who thinks it's time for baby to leave her bottle behind.

- Eliminate first those bottles that are enjoyed the least and replace with a cup. One favorite bottle, such as the one your child drinks while you read her a story, can be kept for as long as she wants.
- Put favorite drinks in a cup and least favored drinks in a bottle.
- Let her continue to drink from the bottle with the nipple and ring removed. Prepare for a mess.

Tommy was 18 months when his mom put away his bottle. He was, however, allowed a bottle at my house — as a special treat. He'd come racing into the house and together we'd hunt out that old bottle. I'd fill it to the brim and he'd carry it around for the whole visit. Seldom did he actually drink out of it. By the time he turned three he tired of our little game, but it was fun while it lasted.

Grandparent

- Let baby practice drinking from a cup while sitting in the bathtub.
- Add thick elastic bands to a glass to give extra grip.

Feeding

- Highchairs have been known to tip over, especially if there is a large dog around. Use a large hook-and-eye fastener and attach the chair to a wall.
- An old shower curtain, rubber bath pad, car mat, or a small stack of newspaper (peel a sheet off after each meal) might be placed under the high chair to collect you-know-what.
- It's not necessary to heat baby food but if you must, use an egg poacher.
- Freeze homemade baby food in sterile ice-cube trays.
- Introduce one new food a week, on a set day. If a child shows an allergic or other reaction to the food, you'll know what the food was and how long it took for the reaction to take place.
- Introduce the new food at the beginning of the meal when baby is very hungry.
- Serve a banana right out of the skin. When baby is full, the rest of the banana can be saved.
- Demi-tasse, tea, or plastic-coated spoons fit into baby's mouth comfortably.
- Give your child a spoon of her own. Sooner or later she will imitate you and feed herself.
- Never give babies brittle plastic picnic utensils. They break easily and small shards may be ingested.

Before my first two kids were born I had this "Leave it to Beaver" idea of what family dinners were supposed to be like. Then I had twins. Perfect dinner? I'd settle for a simple chaotic one.

Parent

- Introduce "soft" baby finger food such as chunks of banana or carrots that have been boiled and cooled when baby is ready to start self-feeding.
- Use a garlic press to turn adult food into baby food.
- If baby slips down in her highchair, try sticking a few bathtub decals on the seat.
- Draw a circle on baby's highchair tray to mark where the cup and/or bowl should go. Baby will have fun trying to put the cup on the spot and will, over time, learn to keep the cup from falling off the tray.
- Choose a highchair that, with tray removed, can be drawn up to the table. Baby will feel that he is part of the family.
- Attach a paper-towel holder to the back of the highchair.
- Place a damp face cloth under baby's food to keep the bowl from slipping.
- To clean a highchair, hose it down and let it stand under the summer sun to dry or stick it in the shower. (Despite your temptation to do otherwise, remove child from high chair first.)
- The hour before dinner is often referred to as "the arsenic hour," as this is the time most child poisonings take place. While you prepare the dinner meal, give hungry kids something to snack on or put out a veggie tray and dip. Use a muffin tin and fill the compartments with different vegetables.

Food to Gnaw On for Teething Babies

Generally, any food that can be squashed between your fingers can be gummed by a six-month-old. Try:

- Frozen bananas (peel banana, wrap in tin foil, and freeze for one hour).
- Rubber toys from the pet store (sterilize them first)
- Bagels — try freezing them

- Dog biscuits
- Cheese chunks
- Fruit juice popsicles (good for sore gums)

Remember, any food can choke a baby. *Never* leave a baby alone with any food. Train your children to sit up straight when eating.

Family Resources in Canada

Family Service Canada (An umbrella organization that lists 50 plus professional agencies across Canada that offer family support. Free.) Contact: Family Service Canada, 55 Parkdale Avenue, Ottawa, Ontario. K1Y 4G1 (613) 728-2463 Fax: (613) 728-3481.

Aid to New Mothers, (Provide referrals and support.)
P.0. Box 84, Station M, Toronto, Ontario. M6S 4T2
(416) 535-2368
New Parent Information Line:
P.O. Box 7282, Oakville, Ontario. L6J C6C
(416) 897-6262

DAYCARE

National Day Care Information Centre, Social Service Program Branch, Health and Welfare, 612 Brooke Claxton Bldg., Tunney's Pasture, Ottawa, Ontario. K1A 1B5. (Provides free information on all aspects of daycare.)

The Canadian Institute of Child Health, 17 York Street, Ottawa, Ontario. K1N 5S7. (613) 238-8425. (Offers a newsletter plus "warm-line".)

The Infant and Toddler Safety Association, 53 Larkspur Crescent, Kitchener, Ontario. N2M 4W8. (519) 579-4863

KidsCanada Publishing Corporation, 542 Mount Pleasant Rd., Toronto, Ontario. M4S 2M7. Publishes yearly directories for Toronto, Calgary and Vancouver ($4.25). Order by calling (416) 481-5696.

U.S.A.

Family Resource Coalition, 230 N. Michigan Ave., Suite 1625, (Dept D) Chicago, IL. 60601. U.S.A. (312) 726-4750. This organization is a clearing house for 500 plus organizations around the country.

Mothers At Home, P.C. Box 2208, Merrifield, VA 22116. U.S.A. (703) 352-2292

PARENT EDUCATION

Consider the following as a "beginners guide" to resources for parents. A call to your local library, information centre, Welcome Wagon, hospital, health services branch may turn up more information for your special needs. And not to forget the obvious — the front of your phone book gives out emergency numbers.

International Planned Parenthood Federation,
Regents College, Inner Circle, Regents Park, London, England. NW1 4NS

Planned Parenthood Federation of Canada,
1 Nicholas Street, Suite 430, Ottawa, Ontario K1N 7B7
(613) 238-4474

Planned Parenthood Federation of America,
810 7th Avenue, New York, NY, U.S.A. 10019
(212) 541-7800

3

Life with Toddlers and Children

The First Bed

Moving toddler from the crib to a single bed can be more traumatic for Mom than child. Alas, she is growing up!

- A pillow may help a toddler center herself.
- Put the mattress on the floor for a few weeks and let your child get used to it.
- "Short-sheet" your child's bed if you'd like to double the protection. Your child's feet will not reach the bottom of the bed anyway.

- Use a toddle guard on the big bed for a few months.
- Put pillows on the floor to soften the fall if she rolls off.
- Wait for the thud.

Toddlers may not sleep well after the big move from crib to bed. Demands for water or stories and frequent potty trips might edge out sleep. In most cases your toddler is simply exerting her new-found freedom, in others she may just be a little nervous about the change. This too will pass.

Sleep and Older Children

As hard as it is to believe, children "enjoy" going to bed on time — they just don't know it. Their body clocks can be set, give or take fifteen minutes or so. Fussing and whining to stay up is not a happy pastime for parent or child. Do them a favor — even if you are a working parent and in an advanced stage of "I-should-spend-more-time-with-them" guilt, make a bedtime schedule and stick to it. Set the pattern and keep it calm. Bath, teeth, PJ's, story, cuddle, that's it!

We work late into the evening and sleep in. Typically, our toddler's regular bedtime and wake-up time is ten o'clock. It works for us!

Parent

- Bed is for rest, not punishment. Chances are children will rebel more at bedtime if they connect bed with bad.
- Beware. A bedtime snack perks kids up rather than settling them down.
- Set a timer or alarm. If bedtime is 8:00, help the child get ready at 7:30. (It takes at least that long if a bedtime story is

involved.) A child may even race the clock to be in bed before it goes off.
- Adult T-shirts may occasionally substitute for PJ's. But remember, while children's nightgowns are by law flame-resistant, all-cotton T-shirts are not.
- If your child doesn't need a full twelve hours a night, have him develop "quiet-time" activities while lying in bed. Let your child read or flip through the pages of a book. Falling into bed with a good book isn't a bad habit to get into.

We have three children. Each child is allowed to stay up later than the others one day of the week. This makes each child feel special and gives my wife and me a chance to catch up with the news of each child.

Parent

Many adult insomniacs can trace their sleep problems back to childhood. Having ruled out any medical problems that may be keeping your little night owl awake (allergies, aches and pains, itches and such), ask yourself if your child is under stress. Most problems resolve themselves but parents can help the process. If your child has real trouble getting to sleep or staying asleep, you might try one or more of these ideas:

- Give your child a very long wind-down time.
- Gear the amount of time slept against her behavior. If she goes to sleep at 9:30, for example, and wakes up refreshed and ready to go at 7:00, then you simply have a child that does not need much sleep. Sleep habits do change, especially during growth spurts.
- A wakeful child at night might need more exercise during the day.

- Give your child a radio to listen to. Provide a headset only if you are sure he will not keep the volume up too loud.
- Don't allow afternoon naps.
- A fish tank is soothing to look at. Add one to a child's room. A nocturnal pet such as a gerbil might also provide a wakeful child with company.
- Talk to your child's doctor.

Night Fears

It's the nature of children to have active imaginations. Would you want your child to be any other way? But although we may understand and accept fears as a natural part of development, they may be hard to deal with night after night.

"As a child I was terrified of my closet. One night my dad came into the room with a broom. He got into the closet and batted my clothes around. He came out disheveled and exhausted and declared "The monster is dead. We laughed, I went to sleep, and that was the end of my monster."

Parent

It's a parent's role to protect and be strong. To dismiss a child's fear is to abdicate the parental role of protector.

- A play sword could be placed under your child's bed for protection.
- A sign reading "No Monsters Allowed" might be hung on the chair.
- Teddy bears have magic powers and can ward off monsters. Make Teddy a sentinel and post him at the closet door.
- Reward your brave child for sleeping through the night.

- Is your child watching scary television? You may want to limit his viewing.

One night our son slept over at a friend's house. We had met the parents and felt comfortable leaving our son with them. However, they allowed the children to watch a teenage horror movie. My son told them that he was not allowed to watch such movies but that didn't seem to make a difference. We had to pick him up at three in the morning.

Parent

Should you read scary fairy tales to young children? Read *The Uses of Enchantment: The Meaning and Importance of Fairy Tales*, Bruno Bettelheim, Vintage Press, for an interesting discussion of this question.

Monsters and bogeymen commonly cause night-time fears but the cause of a child's discomfort may simply be disorientation: everything disappears in the dark or takes on new and ominous proportions.

- Use a night-light (but be careful, night-lights can cast spooky shadows and might make the situation worse).

Safety Note: Night-lights should be functional in their appearance. A night-light that resembles a cartoon figure just begs to be played with. Also, place the light away from the bed to prevent a pillow or blanket from falling over it and creating a fire hazard.

- A fish tank with light makes a good night-light substitute.
- Night visits from a child are easily established but a hard habit to break. If your child is frightened it's best to take her back to her own bed and lie with her for a short while.
- Give your child your pillow to sleep with.

- Use your voice rather than your presence to reassure your child.
- A flashlight tucked under her pillow may be very reassuring.
- Typically, night fears take a quantum leap around Halloween. Be prepared.

Early Risers

At 4:00 a.m. I found my four-year-old manning the VCR. He said there was nothing on television.

Parent

- Do not leave food out for an early riser. A child may lie down to eat, and choke.
- Place a baby gate across the door of your toddler's room if she tends to wander in the wee hours.
- Cover the window with heavy-duty blinds to keep the day out and the night in.
- If you have a job outside the home, early mornings may become your special time together. If you too are an early bird, get up with your child.
- Put an alarm clock in your child's room. Even though your child may not yet tell time, make it a rule that she may not get out of bed until the alarm goes off.
- Leave out safe activities for play (crayons, books, toys).

A Bedroom for an Older Child

Part of going to bed is the bedroom environment. A bedroom must, above all things, be a retreat — a place to relax, read, and sleep. It is also a place that should reflect your child's personality, not your own.

My mother was a decorator and our house was a showcase for her clients. My bedroom was not spared her creative endeavors. If I so much as left books out or put a poster on the wall, my mother had a fit. My friends envied my beautiful room. I hated it.

Parent

- Plan the base of the room and let your child add her own touches. For example, since your child's taste will change from year to year, use a washable, neutral-colored paint or vinyl wallpaper and choose a durable, darkish carpet.
- Furniture should be as accommodating to as many different styles as possible (plain pine as opposed to Louis XIV).
- Opt for shelving that can be moved about to hold toys one day and a stereo system the next.
- Avoid shelving made with planks and bricks. Not only is it ugly, but dangerous as well. Besides, why use up all the college decorating ideas?
- Plain white pull-down blinds can be decorated by a child with paint or markers.
- To change the look of a room instantly buy at least two totally different sets of sheets.
- Don't place hooks at eye level.
- Indoor-outdoor carpeting is durable. Whatever is dropped onto the carpet will be seen, as opposed to shag rug, which can hide pennies and small, swallowable items. It's also easy to clean and flat enough to play cars and trucks on. However, this type of carpeting can cause rugburn on little knees. Weigh the pros and cons.
- A clothesline run across one wall may be used to display artwork, greeting or get well cards, postcards, snapshots, or small posters.

- If you see a particularly nifty shop display that might look neat in your child's room, ask the store manager if you can have it when the display is over. In some cases a display is put into storage but often it's tossed into the garbage. No harm in asking. (If the manager does not wish to keep track of your name, ask when it is to come down and call back on that date.)
- Some (but not all) movie theaters will give away old movie posters. Again, no harm in asking.

When space is tight, layer the children. Buy bunk beds.

- For privacy, make a curtain to surround each bunk.
- Use safety lights (guards over bulbs) above each bunk.
- Make a small fold up mini-table for the-upper bunk.
- Children over six are ready to sleep in the top bunk, assuming your child does not roll out of a regular bed. Safety bars should be on both sides of the bed and the top mattress must be bolted to the upper frame. (No matter how secure the upper mattress is, kids in the lower bunk inevitably kick the upper mattress and dislodge it.)
- Smoke alarms are recommended in all bedrooms but in a room with a bunk bed this recommendation becomes a necessity. Smoke rises and the first person to be overcome is the person in the upper bunk.
- If your children must share a room and if there is a little space, create a small hiding place for each child. This space does not always have to be in the child's room. It just should be private with a light to read by, a blanket plus pillow, and a private box to stash treasures.

Bath Time

Let your children enjoy their bath time. Let them play and splash in the tub, but watch out for bumps and skids with all that water around.

- Turn taps off before allowing a child to climb into the tub.
- To prevent bumps from the faucet cover it with a commercial safety cover. Careful, in some cases the covers collect mold.
- Use a non-skid bath mat.
- Bubble bath has been known to cause vaginal infections. Bubbles are fun, however, and may divert a fearful child.
- A toddler needs no more than a few inches of water.
- Teach your child how to climb out of the tub. Left to their own devices some children will climb up on the lip of the tub and leap.
- If your child is fearful of swirling down the drain, help her out of the tub before pulling the plug.
- To make a bar of soap easy to hold onto, fold a washcloth in half, sew on three snaps, and stick the soap inside the washcloth.
- The best bathtub toys can be found in the kitchen or in the gadget section of a store. Plastic colanders and cups, different-sized bowls, funnels, and short-handled spoons all make great bath toys.
- Store bathtub toys in a net bag or a plastic colander — the holes allow for drainage.
- Commercial bathtub crayons are terrific fun but they will last longer if allowed to dry out completely. Remove them from the muggy bathroom environment after play.
- If your child attends a weekly swim lesson, make the apres-swim shower hair-washing time. Not only will he get rid of that stinky chlorine smell but most children will not kick up a fuss when other kids are around.
- Cut a sponge to fit into the soap dish and eliminate gooey "soft soap syndrome".
- Paint a red dot on the hot faucet as a warning to children. To make sure the faucet is cool to the touch, run cold water through the faucet just before turning off the water. And of course, never run water while a child is in the tub.

When should your child receive bath time privacy? When she demands it! Sure as shootin', one day your child will give you an appalled look as you enter the bathroom and declare, "Mother, can't you see that I'm busy!" Until that moment, keep it a policy to leave bathroom doors open and as a forever-and-ever family policy *never* let a child lock the bathroom door.

Want to keep little people out of the bathroom? Put a sock held in place by an elastic band over the outer handle. Want to keep doors open and prevent crushed fingers? Sling a towel over the top of the door.

Who put the Poo in Shampoo?

Washing hair can be a traumatic experience for kids and parents. The sooner you find the tricks that work, the easier the session will be.

- Help your child wash a doll's hair. Encourage your child to talk to the doll, "Now I'm going to put on the shampoo . . . now I'm going to rub your head" and so on.
- Climb into the bath and let your child help wash your hair.
- A brim that surrounds a child's head and prevents shampoo from dribbling into eyes is available through mail order or in baby stores.
- Give your child a cloth to hold over his eyes while you rinse his head.
- Using swimming goggles or a diving mask is a fun way to keep soap out of eyes.
- Use a small watering can to rinse away shampoo.
- If the shampoo comes out in great globs, pour it into a rinsed-out dish detergent squirt bottle.
- Float the shampoo (and conditioner and/or creams you plan to use after the bath) in the warm bathwater until ready to use.
- Pour shampoo onto a sponge and then put on hair.

- Make hair sculptures with the shampoo. Keep a mirror handy.
- Attach a small hose to the faucet and let your child rinse her own head.
- Sing a song. When the song is over, the shampoo will be too. Or use an egg timer with a bell.
- Introduce your child to the shower. She may prefer it over a bath.
- Always use conditioner on long hair. Otherwise the combing out will be worse than the washing.
- Remove gum from hair by rubbing gum and hair with peanut butter or olive oil. Comb out.
- Watch out for an eye or scalp reaction to the brand of shampoo you are using. In some cases, children have a real reason for hating shampoo time.

After a shampoo we play "hairdresser". I brush out my daughter's hair and set or style it. It was a screaming session before I came up with the name.

Parent

(Little boys could play "barbershop.")

Kids and Food

Picky Eaters

They will survive, no matter how little food seems to pass their lips. From a parent's point of view, a sense of humor and a little creative thinking will make life easier.

- Save TV dinner trays (the kind that divide food into small compartments) for those children who don't like their foods to "touch".

He was six when he started to demand a fork for every type of food on his plate. At one point our son was eating with five forks! It lasted a few months.

Parent

- "Good children leave clean plates" is a philosophy that has had its day. To insist that a child always eat everything on her plate is to invite weight problems later on. Let a child decide when she is full.
- Just for fun serve dinner on a doll tray, a frisbee, or a plastic boat.
- Spread a tablecloth on the floor and have a picnic in the kitchen with your toddler.
- Sometimes children will gobble down their dinner to see the picture embossed on the plate.
- Give out small dollops of food rather than full plates and encourage children to ask for seconds. A massive amount of food set in front of a child is intimidating.
- Use cookie cutters to cut bread into shapes (butterflies, circles, triangles) and melt cheese over them.
- The more a child is exposed to different foods, the more likely she is to try them. A child may be willing to have "strange" food sit on her plate but may refuse to eat it. Time is on your side.
- Children differentiate between tasting and swallowing. It's not uncommon for a child to test the food in her mouth and spit it out. This is not a behavior to be encouraged but don't be surprised when it happens.
- Kids often dislike stews because they cannot identify the different ingredients. Have your child don a chef's apron and help you in food preparation. He can then inspect each item as it is popped into the pot.

- What to serve a picky eater? Dump the problem on your child. Let him plan a balanced lunch once a week. Graduate him to planning, and finally to helping cook, one family meal a week.
- Tape up a few holes on the salt shaker to prevent children from dumping on too much salt. (That's assuming you have not chosen to ban it altogether.)

My daughter hated boiled eggs until my mom showed her that age-old trick — how to fool her mom by eating the egg, turning the shell upside down, and then saying, "Mommy, I won't eat this egg." That's my cue to get mad. "Surprise," she yells as she turns over the empty shell, "All gone." It works every time.

Parent

- Let your child choose "additives" for soups, such as cheese slices, an egg, frozen vegetables, sliced wieners. (If you add them yourself, the soup will be unacceptable.)
- Have your children list the food they like and try using the base ingredients in other ways; for example, if they like pasta perhaps you could try different sauces.
- Who says spaghetti can't be eaten for breakfast? Put last night's leftovers (noodles and sauce) on a microwave-safe tray and pop them into the microwave in the morning to reheat. Hamburgers, pizza, and fish are also tasty in the morning.
- Serve dry cereal, with milk, in a cup. The leftover milk can be drunk.
- Collect the last bits of cereal left in the bottom of boxes and mix them in a bowl for a nuts and bolts treat or put them all in one box for a "surprise" mixed cereal. You can even put them in sandwich-size bags and pop them in lunch boxes.

- "If you can't dip it, it's not food" — the credo of the North American kid. Serve raw vegetables with a yogurt-based dip as an after-school snack.
- Rename food. Broccoli may be called "little trees," for example. ("My goodness, Billy, you ate the whole tree, trunk, branches, leaves, and all!") Call a raw vegetable plate "wabbit food." Fish sticks might be called "fish candy" and anything round may be a version of a cookie.
- Introduce chopsticks. Chinese chopsticks are bigger than the Japanese and therefore easier to handle. Tape the ends of the chopsticks together. Take an inch of cardboard and fold in half. Put the cardboard between the sticks. They will now behave like giant tweezers and will be easier to manipulate.

When she bursts into the house after school I know that she will eat almost anything. I make up a mini plate of cheese, raw veggie sticks, sliced apples, and all the other food that she normally wouldn't touch. Knowing when your child is hungry helps.

Parent

- Let your child make limited choices at the food market. "We have to buy a tin of peas. Of these three tins which one should we buy?"
- Children go through food phases. One child may seem to eat nothing but peanut butter for a month, another may only eat hotdogs. In young children these phases disappear as suddenly as they appear.
- Adults may unconsciously steer children away from "adult" food on the assumption that they won't like it. Let children develop their own tastes. (Believe it or not, at the moment my son dislikes all cheese but blue cheese.)

- Serve cold water from a colorful jug. Pour into colorful glasses.
- Forget soda pop. Carbonated water mixed with a tablespoon of condensed frozen orange juice (or grape, or lemonade, or whatever) makes a much tastier drink.
- If your picky eater is driving you crazy at the dinner table, make a conscious effort to steer the conversation to topics other than food.
- Demanding perfect table manners is asking too much. On the other hand, if your child keeps getting up from the table during a meal, make a rule: leave the table and your dinner is finished.
- Fill a flat-bottomed ice cream cone with fruits, vegetables, salad or anything you can think of.

Breakfast was an egg on a muffin. Lunch — a hamburger. For dinner I served a vegetable plate plus dip, chicken strips with dip, and french fries. By writing down our typical daily menus, I realized that my kids were not only missing out on nutrients but they seldom had to use a knife and fork! No wonder kids today have such poor table manners.

Parent

Occasionally a picky eater develops serious eating disorders. Talk to your doctor.

Lunch-Box Blues

- Rule Number One: If your child won't eat it at home, he most certainly will not eat it at school!
- If your child is turned off by lunch-box lunches try packing a lunch with a theme. Choose a color theme — today all lunch ingredients must be orange — a salmon sandwich, carrot

sticks, cheddar cheese chunks, a tangerine, peach yogurt, etc. How about a "shape" theme? Everything in the lunch must be triangular. Or use stickers to decorate all the items at Christmas or Halloween or Easter.

- Pop a juice box in the freezer the night before, wrap it in plastic (to prevent sweating), and put it at the bottom of the box. It will keep the rest of the food cool.
- Use frozen bread slices in warm weather. The bread will defrost by lunchtime and, meanwhile, it will keep the filling cool.
- Flatten plain bread with a rolling pin and smear on the peanut butter and jam. Now roll up the sandwich and slice. Interesting, no? (Well, your child may think so.)
- Put peanut butter in a hotdog bun (whole wheat if you prefer). Add a banana to the lunch. All your child has to do is peel the banana and put it inside the bun. Ta-da, a peanut butter and banana bun!
- Sandwiches are not lunch-box necessities, no matter what we have been taught. A chunk of cheese, a cracker or two, a milk shake, and a veggie stick are as good or better than a soggy peanut butter sandwich.
- If your child loves cereal, put a serving in a plastic container and add the appropriate amount of dried milk. Show your child how much tap water to add. Stir and presto! Breakfast for lunch! (If you haven't tried dried milk in years, try it again. It's improved.) Of course, you could always send milk along in a thermos.
- Teach children to pack up their own lunches. They must be told to wash their hands before touching any food.
- Set a specific time aside, Sunday night, for example, and make the week's sandwiches together. Freeze them. To identify the sandwiches easily cut them differently. For example, cut salmon sandwiches in half, egg on the diagonal, and so on.
- Instead of sending an edible treat, write out a joke. "What's the only room a person can never go into? A mushroom!"

(Find a good joke book and keep it in reserve.) It's not usually a good idea to put mushy "I love you" notes in a lunch box. The note may fall into the wrong hands.

Safety Note: Careful with the plastic bags. Children must be taught not to treat them like balloons or suck on them to make a popping sound. If ingested, plastic bags, like balloons, contour to a child's throat and may cause suffocation.

Most thermoses do not keep meat-based soups hot enough to prevent bacterial growth.

- Rather than advertising your child's name on her lunch box, add stickers for easy identification.
- On the first day of school, tape a funny family picture on the inside of the box in case your child gets a little homesick.
- Use brown bags only once, as they may become contaminated.
- One can easily spot a mom at the condiment counter in a fast-food restaurant — she's the one loading up on little packets of pepper and mustard. A more honest alternative is to save plastic pill or film roll containers with twist-on tops. Fill them with condiments.

I started to hear comments from volunteer mothers at the school like "My goodness, your daughter doesn't eat much lunch." Finally her teacher told me that one day my daughter turned up at school with only an apple in her lunch box. She was eating her lunch on the bus.

Parent

- Keep lunch or milk money to a minimum. A child who regularly walks around flashing cash may be bullied. Tape quarters to the inside lid of the lunch box. Collect quarters in

a kitchen jar and divide into little packets every Monday. Sew a "hidden" pocket in your child's school coat just for emergency/lunch/milk money.
- Include a mid-morning or bus snack in the lunch.
- No matter how much effort you put into preparing a balanced lunch-box meal, your child is bound to trade off most of it anyway. Add a bag of "tradable" or coveted treats: a mini-bag of dried Captain Crunch cereal, an extra fruit roll-up, a small bag of popcorn.

My son's teacher puts a large bowl on her desk after lunch. The kids fill it with leftover food they would otherwise have tossed out, such as apples, oranges, and other good stuff. At 2:30 they have a mid-afternoon break and the children are invited to pick through the bowl. What was unappetizing at 12:00 is delicious a couple of hours later.

Parent

In most schools the children eat lunch and then go out to play. The inevitable results are that kids plow through their food and end up running around on full stomachs. Suggest that the school change its policy.

After-School Snacks

This can be the most important meal of your child's day. Try some of the following suggestions to make sure that your child is not filling up on sugary or fatty foods.

- Apple and orange slices, cheese chunks, a carrot, two cookies, and a jelly baby all arranged on a plate make for a great snack.

- Prepare zip-lock bags of snacks and leave them in the fridge.
- A bowl of dried cereal may be just what your child needs.
- Top a slice of English muffin with spaghetti sauce (out of a jar) and a cheese slice for an instant pizza.
- Wash any fruit that your child might grab straight out of the fridge.

4

Medical Matters

When Children Get Sick

"Mommy, I feel sick." Bets are Mom suddenly feels a heck of a lot worse than child! Chin up — colds and the flu are part of the game and chances are you'll both survive although child may fare better than parent.

The Medicine Chest

Here's a list of things you should always have on hand at home.

- Nasal aspirator
- Thermometer

- Petroleum jelly
- Oral dosing syringe and/or a calibrated spoon
- Liquid aspirin substitute
- Syrup of Ipecac
- Antiseptic cream
- Bandaids, gauze, and first-aid tape
- Tweezers
- Sunscreen (Note: Sunscreen should not be applied to an infant under six months old.)

Doctors and Dentists

Finding a Pediatrician

What are your requirements? If you don't have a car forget about that "fabulous doc" across town. You may want a doctor who holds "telephone" hours. (Ask about extra costs.) Choose one who practices what she preaches; for example, a jargon-spouting type who does not talk directly to infants and children is not for you. You may prefer a doctor who is connected with an accessible hospital and who is certified by such organizations as The Canadian Pediatric Society or The American Academy of Pediatrics. Most important, choose a doctor who boosts you up, who makes you feel like a worthwhile and capable parent, who asks you general questions about your life (as it effects your baby's), and who makes you smile.

Make up a short list of potential candidates by:

- Asking some nurses. If they won't give you opinions on Dr. X then ask who they take their kids to.
- Having a chat with a midwife or a midwifery organization.
- Attending a La Leche meeting while in the prenatal stage and asking for recommendations.
- Talking to friends who have children or to other parents at a play school or day care.
- Asking for several referrals from your obstetrician/gynecologist or family doctor.

THE INTERVIEW

Some doctors charge for an initial interview, others do not. Ask when phoning for an appointment. When you go to the interview take mental notes. Ask yourself:

- What is the atmosphere of the waiting room like?
- Is the receptionist pleasant? Is the nurse friendly?
- What is the usual wait in the office? (Ask other patients.)
- How are emergencies handled?
- Is the doctor's practice "shared" with other doctors? Can you meet these other doctors?
- What are the doctor's opinions on breast-feeding, circumcision, nutrition? Write out your list of topics in advance.
- Does the doctor communicate well with you?

Many of these questions seem excessive but no one needs surprises during an emergency. Besides, this is a relationship that may continue for the next sixteen years or more.

CHILD MEETS DOCTOR

Bring a notepad and pencil with you to the doctor's office. (You will forget the instructions you are given.) Bring an extra diaper for a baby. Upon arrival, ask if the doctor is seeing patients on time. If there is a long delay and the weather is fine, you may want to take your child for a stroll rather than wait in an office crowded with sick kids. (Technically, the doctor will see all contagious children immediately and they will not be left to play with other kids in the waiting room. If you think your child is contagious, tell the nurse.)

Doctors should talk directly to toddlers. The doctor will ask you for specifics but the doctor that treats your child as if he were a mute log is telling you something.

If you are seeking a second opinion, do not give out the first doctor's diagnosis immediately as this may consciously or otherwise sway the second diagnosis.

Dentist Shopping

Most children make their first visit to the dentist before they are two and a half (check with your dentist on his/her preference). A first appointment usually involves little more than a ride in the chair and a "look-see" in the mouth. A dentist who keeps a mini treasure trove of penny gifts really knows what he/she is doing.

Finding a dentist involves much the same detective work as finding a baby doctor and it's just as important a search. The most prevalent mistake parents make is to assume that their dentist will be suitable. Seldom is a dentist specializing in children necessary, but dentists who are prepared to handle very young children are a rare breed.

When you go for a visit, look around and ask yourself:

- Does the waiting room look as if children are welcome as opposed to tolerated?
- Are the receptionist and dental assistant pleasant?
- Does the dentist take time to explain procedures to the child as well as to you?
- Will the dentist explain dental hygiene to your child?
- Are parents allowed to stay with children during the examination?
- Under what conditions will a dentist send a child to a dental specialist (in particular, ask about orthodontal work).
- How does the doctor wish to be paid? Some bill per appointment, others monthly.

DENTAL CARE

- Children often complain that adult toothpaste "burns" Switch to a paste formulated for kids.
- Encourage flossing. Tear off a foot (30 cm) of the floss, loop it, and tie. It will now be easier to use.
- Start a routine. Rinse (gargle with water), floss, brush, rinse.
- Most adult mouthwash contains large amounts of alcohol. Keep it out of reach of children.

- Keep an egg timer by the toothbrushes. When the sand runs out dental care is finished.
- Electric toothbrushes are recommended for children with dexterity problems.
- Let children pick their own color of brush.
- Let your child practice brushing her teeth in the tub.
- Mount a mirror at tooth level.
- Raisins, which are often tossed into lunch boxes, are a good source of potassium and other vitamins and minerals but they do stick to teeth and cause cavities. Reduce their cavity-causing potential by giving your child a chunk of cheddar cheese, a handful of peanuts, sunflower seeds, or a carrot or apple.
- If your baby develops a case of thrush (a yeast infection of the mouth caused by an organism called *Candida*), check to see if her pacifier is the culprit. This organism can be transferred to the pacifier and ping-pong back again.

THE TOOTH FAIRY COMETH

- Remind children that the tooth fairy gives more for a clean tooth than for a decayed one.
- Drop your child's tooth into a pill container before tucking it under the pillow. Loose teeth get lost.
- A note from the tooth fairy congratulating your child on her perfect teeth might encourage her to keep up the good work.
- Sprinkle the pillow with sparkles (fairy dust).

Fear of the Doctor or Dentist

Children between the ages of one and three, and sometimes beyond, commonly experience stranger anxiety. The unfamiliar environment of a waiting room and the approaching stranger dressed in a lab coat may frighten even a normally inquisitive child. Previous painful experiences (needles or tests) may contribute to your child's anxiety. Most baby doctors have their own ways and means of handling this fear but a parent can help.

- Bring along a doll and ask the doctor to give the doll a quick examination beforehand.
- Try to limit the stay in the waiting room. Call ahead if a long delay is typical.
- Bring along a bottle, books, or toys to occupy your child.
- Don't use illness as a threat; for example, "If you don't eat your dinner you will get sick and I'll have to take you to the doctor."
- Try not to let your child overhear Granny's descriptive commentary on her operation. And dentures left in plain sight can unnerve anyone, let alone a child.
- Avoid making demeaning or sarcastic comments about medical or dental people in the presence of your child.
- Buy your child a doctor's kit. She may not play with it immediately but if it's around she might gravitate to it when ready.

A fear of the dentist may be passed from parent to child or from sibling to sibling. The days of painful needles and toe-curling sessions in the dental chair are a thing of the past. It's not uncommon to see youngsters looking forward to the dentist! Let children form their own opinions.

Bumps, Bruises, and Scrapes

- After putting a bandaid on an infant, cover it with clothing. Infants eat bandaids. If the bandaid must go on the face, trim her nails and cover her hands with mitts.
- Bandaids decorated with clown or happy faces may ease the hurt. Draw one on with a marker.
- A bandaid placed on Teddy or Dolly may make child feel that the ouch is shared.
- If the antiseptic threatens to sting, wash the cut and put the antiseptic on the bandaid rather than on the sore.
- When it's time to remove the bandaid, dab mineral or baby oil over it for an ouchless removal.

- Protect a hurt finger from further bumps by making a splint out of two popsicle sticks or putting the finger into a hair roller.
- To keep the screaming to a minimum have the child describe the pain in an exact way or describe how she got hurt. Tell her it's okay to cry but for the moment you have work to do; promise to make time for crying in a few minutes. Ask her to whistle, let her blow a whistle, or have her count out loud.
- Tennis wrist bands make great knee protectors for little crawlers. An adult wrist band can also act as a soft "cast" for a scraped shin.

My son is terrified of blood. One day he had a nosebleed and I gave him a roll of paper towels. He took one look at all that red blood on the white tissue and nearly passed out. I ran to the bathroom and gave him a red, damp facecloth. He felt much better once the blood "disappeared".

Parent

- A bag of frozen vegetables, a popsicle, or a can of frozen juice make good instant ice packs.
- To give eye drops, pull the bottom lid of the eye down gently until it forms a little pocket. Drop in a drop. It's not a good idea to have the drops touch the outer part of the eye but if you are desperate, gently clean the eyelid with a facecloth and have the child lie down and close her eyes. Place the drops in the corner of her eye. Now tell her to open her eyes. The drops will roll in.
- If a child's eye is injured and medical emergency services recommend that you rinse the eye, have the child lie on his side with the injured eye closest to the ground. Gently drip

the water down over the eye. (This method will ensure that the other eye remains uncontaminated.)

- Remove a splinter in the finger by first running it under water or apply a bit of ice. The splinter may stand and show itself.

  Or dab with iodine and the splinter will appear as a dark sliver. Itty-bitty splinters such as cactus spines can be removed easily if you first dab on a bit of clear paper glue. Peel the glue off and the splinters will come off too.
- If your child is to receive a needle, don't minimize the pain but do tell her how long the pain will last — "When I count to ten it will be all over."

When my firstborn fell down, my husband and I would encourage him to keep a stiff upper lip. Seldom did we sympathize and hug. We were hoping to instill a certain toughness to pain. One day his little brother fell off his bike and hurt himself badly. My older son stood and watched, told him to get up and stop crying, and then he walked away. He's tough all right, but not very sympathetic to others. We have changed our ways!

Parent

Sticks and Stones and Broken Bones

- Never allow a child to poke a knitting needle or any other sharp object down into a cast to relieve itching. An inadvertent scratch might become infected and cause a whole new set of problems.
- Blow warm air from a hand-held hair dryer down into a cast to soothe itching.
- Rub petroleum jelly on the skin at either end of the cast to prevent chafing.

- To clean up a cast, roll on white shoe polish.
- If your child strongly objects to using crutches, decorate them. (Pop into a sewing center or craft store and have some fun.)

Keeping Out the Cold

It's not unusual for a child to have as many as ten colds a year, especially if this is her first year in day care, play school, or kindergarten. Children who are otherwise thriving will develop immunities.

- Most colds occur in the winter, thanks to overheated, dry, poorly ventilated rooms. Unless it is very cold outside wrap the kids up and send them out to play.
- Wash hands frequently. Introduce your family to the twenty-second scrub. Remember, it's not soap that kills viruses. Soap removes the germs and water carries them away. And keep kids' nails neat and short.
- Soap in a pump is sanitary and easy to handle.
- Stuffed toys harbor germs, which is why they are not recommended for day care. The flip side to this is that children sometimes need the comfort of a stuffed pal. The solution for home and day care — buy or use stuffed animals that can be "skinned" and washed. Stuffed toys that can only be surface washed should probably not be shared.
- Covering a sneeze with a hand can spread the cold, especially if that hand is next used to touch another person. Teaching a child to let it fly is a disgusting alternative. Poke kleenex up his sleeve (like Granny does hers) as a matter of habit during the cold season. (Few small children, however, have the dexterity to retrieve the kleenex pre-sneeze. Therefore, after a sneeze it's into the bathroom for a hand wash.)
- Paper towels and kleenex are preferable to handkerchiefs.
- Banish the communal bathroom water glass. Use disposable paper cups or assign one labeled plastic glass to each person.

- Toothbrushes harbor germs. No sharing! Change them every three months, more often during the cold season.
- Color-code your bathroom. Give Jenny a yellow toothbrush, a yellow hand towel, and a yellow bathroom bag to stash her bathroom stuff in. Billy's bathroom set might be purple.
- Is this a familiar picture? Two or more spaghetti-sauce-dipped little faces sit at the kitchen table. Mom takes a facecloth and within seconds makes history of those orange grins. Oops! What a great way to spread germs. Get rid of the communal facecloth.

When Colds or the Flu Arrive

- Call the doctor. Keep notepaper and a pencil near the phone and jot down any concerns you may have or symptoms your child may be showing. It's a sure bet that you'll forget most things when the call to, or from, the doctor gets through.
- Offer fluids, fluids, and more fluids. Flat ginger ale is a perennial favorite, especially with those children who normally are not allowed pop.
- If your child refuses to drink, try throwing a mini-tea-party, buy pretty, wiggly straws that beg to be tried, offer strong fruit-flavored drinks, or hand out popsicles or ice cubes.

Temperatures

Should you give your child a pill at the first sign of a fever? There is increasing evidence to suggest that fever helps the body battle nasty germs. Talk to your child's doctor about this pill-popping behavior *before* your child develops a fever.

Keep in mind that a child with a low temperature could be very ill, while a high temperature may not indicate a serious problem. What usually counts is your child's behavior and "look." Furthermore, while temperature patterns do differ, most kids' temperatures tend to go up at night. (All the better to worry you with.) On the other hand, an infant under six months with a temperature does need medical attention.

- When taking a temperature, opt for a digital thermometer. They are not wildly expensive and are fast and accurate.
- Rectal thermometers are the alternative for infants and toddlers. Be sure to apply petroleum jelly to the tip before gently inserting it. Move on to oral thermometers as soon as your child can keep it under her tongue.
- If your child refuses to keep a thermometer in her mouth for the duration, let her time herself with the help of a kitchen egg timer.
- Sing a song your child knows. Tell her that the thermometer will be ready at the end of the song.

Stuffy Noses

A nasal bulb or, if your child is under a year, a small ear syringe helps remove nasty mucus that clogs the nose. If necessary loosen the mucus with a saline solution (a pinch of salt in a cup of water or buy a commercial solution). Never use adult nose drops on a child without consulting a doctor. Remember, it's normal to have mucus in the nose and, for that matter, a little ear wax in the ear. Don't go overboard with the cleaning. Note: A bulb must be thoroughly cleaned or it will become a hotbed of germs.

Giving Medicine

- To take the edge off medicine that tastes ghastly, chill it in the fridge. An ice cube may help desensitize a child's taste buds.
- Drop the medicine in a nipple and give it to your infant just before feeding time.
- Use an oral dosing syringe for infants under six months. (Measure the dose, load the syringe, and place it gently inside baby's cheek. Do not give any liquids to a baby that is lying down.)
- Give medicine before a feeding unless directed otherwise.
- Avoid mixing with food, as some foods will lessen the effects of the medication.

- If you must administer more than one medication, let your child pick the order.
- Be matter-of-fact about the whole thing. Pleading or bargaining with a child implies that he has a choice and he may refuse the medicine.
- *Never* mix medicine with a bottle of juice. If baby does not drink all of the juice, you'll have no idea how much was actually ingested.
- Chewable pills are a blessing but at some point children must be taught how to swallow a pill. Have your child put the pill at the back of her throat and swallow a gulp of water. If the pill won't go down, try coating it very lightly with salad oil. As a last resort, crush it between two spoons and serve it up with a dollop of pudding.
- If your child is having trouble breathing, raise the head of the bed by stashing a few books under the top legs. Or prop the mattress up with the help of folded blankets. Another idea — haul out a lawn lounge chair that adjusts to different positions.
- Gargling is fun and messy. Let your child practice with water. Consider carefully before giving your child an adult commercial gargle. Children may be put off by that "refreshing" taste; in a few cases the gargle may upset a child's stomach, and some gargles contain an inordinate amount of alcohol.
- A muggy bathroom is no place to keep medication for any length of time.
- Stash medication that requires refrigeration in an opaque container at the back of the fridge. (No one, least of all a child is likely to open a container that looks like it may harbor green, growing gunk.)
- If you must transport medicine on a regular basis (to and from the cottage, for example), lock it up in a metal fishing tackle box. (In a hotel the box may double as a bathroom step stool.) Do not keep medication in the glove compartment. On a summer's day the car's interior may become extremely

hot. If you must leave medicine in the car for a short time, store it under a newspaper on the floor or under the seat.

- Jumbo T-shirts from your wardrobe make good bedclothes for sick kids. They will not constrict movement, they are easily washed, there is usually an endless supply, and they are fun to wear.
- A bell placed beside a child's bed to summon dear Mama just begs to be abused. Nevertheless, a little ringing is preferable to screams up and down the stairs. (Note: Do not substitute a bell with a whistle. Young children can confuse blowing in with blowing out.)
- Children get heartburn too. A peppermint might quell the pain.
- A blanket tossed into the dryer for a few minutes will give snugly comfort and quieten down a rambunctious child.

My three- and five-year-old share a room. During the night I left cough medicine beside my five-year-old's bed. My three-year-old drank the bottle.

Parent

- How to tell if your asthmatic child's inhaler is empty? Remove the mouthpiece and plunk the cartridge in a full glass of water. A full inhaler will sink to the bottom and lie there, an empty one will float on its side.

Bored and Bed-bound

Occupying a sick child is much easier if there is money to spare; a mini computer or games that hook up to the TV will usually occupy older children for hours on end. However, even these games can pall after a while. A little creativity is in order.

- Make your own activity bag. Cut out a few pictures from discarded coloring books and glue them on cardboard. Offer three crayons or a select number of washable markers. Add blunt scissors, paper plates, bits of material, and a child's magazine.
- Make a worktable out of a cookie sheet or tray. The lip on the tray will prevent crayons from rolling off. Stash crayons and markers in a covered plastic freezer container.
- An ironing board makes a neat eating tray or worktable. Or take a cardboard box and cut out leg holes to form a tray.
- Room service can make an illness bearable, at least from your child's point of view. To keep dishes from sliding all over the tray, place them on a damp facecloth. After the meal use the cloth to wipe a grubby face.
- Keep a thermos filled with cold drinking water in your child's room. She may be too young to pour but you'll find it handy.
- Give your child your old wedding or family album to peruse and laugh at.

My four-year-old was bed-ridden for months. At the foot of his bed I posted a medical chart where we recorded meals and sleep time. I made two medical gowns out of old shirts for my six- and eight-year-old. After school the kids would rush up to play with their brother.

Parent

Long-Term Care

Try to balance your concern with the child's needs. Sympathy gone awry may convince the child that he is best loved when sick. On the other hand, everyone loves and needs a little extra attention when ill.

- Hang a bird feeder directly outside the bedroom window. Give her a bird book and binder to log the different types of feathered friends that come to visit. (Suggested books: *Birdwise*, Pamela M. Hickman, Kids Can Press; *Bird Watch*, Mary MacPherson, Summerhill Press; or *The Bird Book*, by Neil and Karen Dawn, Somerville House.)
- Now might be the time to introduce a new hobby — collect stickers, stamps, postcards, get-well cards, or other treasures in a large photograph album.
- An ant farm, gold fish, or the neighbor's hamster will provide company.

Children, like adults, need to be needed. When my eight-year-old was bed-ridden with a very nasty leg break we adapted a few chores to suit his disability. He sorted and matched socks, typed letters (sort of), polished silverware, and became our own house secretary (answering the phone, taking messages). I even gave him the job of calling PTA members to remind them about meetings. We discovered plenty of jobs he could do.

Parent

- Drop into the local library and stock up on story-telling cassettes.
- Subscribe, in your child's name, to some magazines. *Owl* and *Chickadee* are two award-winning magazines that offer activities as well as stories.
- Make a windowsill garden. Start with a paper cup, punch holes in the bottom, fill with potting soil, and plant seeds. (Draw a face on the cup, plant grass, and the "face" will grow a head of hair.)

- A two-way transistor might make your bed-bound child feel like he is still part of the action.
- Change your child's room around to give her a different perspective. (Don't worry about the practicality of the arrangement, it's only temporary.)
- Make up a daybed in the family room. (If your child is able to travel from room to room, transport her toys and books in a small plastic laundry basket.)
- Change her bed often to get rid of that sickly feel.
- If your child is to be in bed for a long time, ask your librarian or local resource center for ideas. Your child may become involved in a Read-A-Thon, for example.
- Keep in touch with your child's school.
- Encourage your child to telephone her school chums. (A five-year-old's telephone conversation may prove wanting but that's okay.)
- Establish a pattern as soon as possible; for example, change or make the bed every morning at 9:00, watch TV until 10:00 (otherwise called Mom's time out), arts and crafts until 11:00, and so on. Write it down.

My four-year-old was in bed for three long months. We were all depressed. One day I brought home a "Three Stooges" video. I know that in today's world some may consider the Three Stooges as unsuitable material for a four-year-old, but it made us laugh. We'd cozy up in bed, block out the sun, and watch them for hours. I'm not suggesting that laughter is everyone's cure but it was for us.

Parent

- Take a jumbo calendar (the kind banks sometimes give out) and write daily activity ideas that suit your child's disability.

Add stickers, jokes, and drawings. Or, take a daily planner and do the same thing but don't allow your child to turn more than one page at a time.

Caring for a sick child over a long time is unbelievably stressful. Plan for time out. Hire a preteen to entertain your child while you read a book. And I know this sounds easy and isn't, but don't ignore the rest of the family. Your sick child needs them too and after awhile they may come to resent their sick sibling.

Every family should have an up-to-date resource book on prescriptive and nonprescriptive drugs.

A Child in Hospital

Suggestions like "Don't be intimidated by medical professionals" and "When it comes to your children's health, trust your instincts" are easily rhymed off and easily dismissed. However, if you don't make yourself heard, it may cost your child's life. I speak from experience.

My own son was two years old when we rushed him to the hospital. He had been projectile vomiting since birth but doctor after doctor told us "it was nothing." The night came when we knew they were wrong.

Four doctors tried to convince us that our son had the flu. We insisted he be hospitalized. I stayed with my son that night. He was very seriously ill and I knew it. Ten hours after admission, a full forty-eight hours after this episode had begun, I threw a tantrum that would have gained me the respect of every two-year-old in the country. Doctors stood and stared and all but one nurse tsk-tsked. That nurse said, "She's right."

An hour later my son's bowel intussusception was diagnosed. Two hours later he was in emergency surgery.

From the bottom of my heart I tell you — trust yourself. Stand up to an entire hospital if you have to. At the very worst you'll only embarrass yourself. (Never mind, embarrassment is part of the parent ball game.) But you may be saving your child's life.

True, our instincts can occasionally go awry. Ask yourself: Am I reacting to the situation, to my fears, or to my child's needs? Do I know my child's personality? Sometimes what stands between children and chance is a stubborn parent. Stand tall!

Hospital Life

- If a hospital stay is planned, ask about pre-admission and a orientation tour with your child.
- Some children may perceive illness and the hospital as punishment, especially if they are admitted because of an accident. Separation from the family may confirm these feelings. Talk about it.
- Ask for help from mental-health professionals. If your child was involved in an accident that resulted in the death of another, he will feel guilty. On the other hand, if you, as a parent, feel the accident was "your fault" then you should seek support, not only for yourself but for the sake of your child.
- Fantasy is often more terrifying than reality. Be honest with your child from the beginning. If he asks "Will it hurt?" and the answer is yes, tell him so. More important, tell him how long the pain will last; for example, "The needle will hurt for a few seconds. Count to ten with me."
- Describe the events as they are about to happen and not hours or days before. It's not necessary to tell a child about the barium enema that is to take place tomorrow, but it is important to tell her about it just before it happens.
- A parent's fear is transferable. Hold it in check by keeping informed. Keep a running list of questions for the doctor. Never let any person dismiss or trivialize your questions.
- Keep a pad and pen with you always. Jot down the names of your child's attending physician (the person responsible for

your child) and the names of all those involved in your child's care, including nurses and assistants.

- Hospital staff are not the enemy, nor are they your best buddies. They are professionals, your child's medical caretakers, and your information resource.
- If you are to get around the hospital rules, you'll need to know them well. Read all the available brochures.

One night I snuck in a box of cookies, pop, comic books, and a flashlight. All of these foods were allowed but they were more delicious since they were eaten on the sly and under covers. We giggled for an hour. We had a wonderful time.

Parent

- "It's against the rules" is a phrase you'll hear often (and a pox on anyone who says it). If the rules seem unreasonable try not to get defensive. Ask why. If they are designed for the convenience of the staff rather than the welfare of your child, then question them. (Many large children's hospitals have a parents' advocacy group. Ask.)
- Inquire about the in-house services and those offered nearby. (Where is the nearest bank machine? What in-house educational facilities are there for children?)
- Make friends with other parents.
- Keep a roll of quarters on hand for coffee and telephone calls.
- You have the right to demand a change in doctor/nurse care if you feel that a particular person is not meeting the needs of your child. But rather than alienate the staff, talk over your concerns with the head nurse before making demands.
- Unless otherwise stated, it's best to dress your child in his or her own labeled PJ's. Hospital gear can be scary. If possible

dress your child in day clothes during the day to convey the message of normality.

- A young child may appreciate a doctor's kit while an older child might like to handle a real stethoscope. (But be careful, stethoscopes can come apart and the hose might pose a hazard to young children.)
- Use reassuring, positive names for scary equipment. A stethoscope might be called Winny-the-Worm for example.
- Decorate your child's crib or bed with pictures from home.
- With the endless amount of poking and probing, children, like adults, may lose a sense of identity and control in the hospital. Respect their space. Don't hop up on the bed without permission or shift toys and cards around to suit yourself.
- It may not be possible to take a child out for a walk but you may be able to take her down to the gift shop or to a solarium. (The object is not to expose her to every germ in the hospital so ask before charging down the halls.)
- Take Pictures of your child at different stages of recovery. Not only will your child begin to see her improvement but she'll be able to take them to show-and-tell once back at school.

My little girl was so sick that I didn't want anyone bothering her with school studies. Despite this, her teacher convinced me to allow a half hour of "school" each day. My daughter actually perked up! I think the lessons helped because she believed that only kids who are going to get better need to learn.

Parent

- If you can't "live-in" with your child, record a few stories on a cassette for nighttime listening. Upbeat stories that are neither sad nor scary are the obvious choice. Repeat that you love her and that you will see her in the morning. (Note: there's a decent chance a cassette recorder will be pinched in hospital. Leave a cheap one with your child, label it, and be prepared to replace it.)

- If the hospital stay will be lengthy and your child is in school, make arrangements for a tutor. (The hospital or your school board will help here.) If a tutor is out of the question, talk with your child's teacher about homework.

Your child's hospital bag should include:

- Several pairs of PJ's and a housecoat
- Slippers
- A change of daytime clothes
- Pillow (label it with a black felt pen)
- Cheerful pillow-cases
- Flashlight
- Walkman or radio with earplugs
- Toys and books
- Pictures of family members
- Loose change for the phone (no bills)
- Daily diary
- List of phone numbers (home, work, Grandma, best friend)

Label everything and don't get upset if a few things are mislaid or pinched.

Live-In Parents

More progressive hospitals allow and even encourage parents to sleep over in the child's hospital room. Other commitments may make such an arrangement unsuitable but if possible stay with your child, especially during those first terrifying nights.

- Wear a cheerful jogging suit with sneakers. Constricting pants or a skirt may not let you have those all-important catnaps and noisy or squeaky shoes will not endear you to staff or patients.

- Depending on the sleeping arrangements, bag a cot early in the day and be prepared to rise early; "rounds" may start at 6:30. Ask.

When I stayed over in hospital I noticed a little boy in the bed across from my daughter's. He was three years old and very scared. In the middle of the night I brought a few books over and read to him for two hours. Finally, with a big smile, he drifted off to sleep. I found out the next day that he didn't speak a word of English.

Parent

- Where can you take a shower and freshen up? Hospital staff may not appreciate your having a dip in the patients' tub.
- Keep your personal paraphernalia down to a minimum and do not keep any valuables or large amounts of money with you.
- What are the cafeteria hours? (If limited food is allowed in the room, stock up on fruit juice in disposable, single containers.)
- What can you do to participate in your child's care? (Change diapers, spoon-feed, etc.) If you have had medical training, speak up. State your commitment to your child's care.
- Older children will need time out from hovering parents and a parent should encourage independence even in a hospital. Let them go to the playroom alone. If they dress themselves at home, let them dress themselves in the hospital. Don't talk about "what's good for them" all the time.
- When others come to visit, especially your child's friends, use that time to take a breather. Go shopping, take in a movie, have a nap.
- Let family and friends spell you.

My seven-year-old daughter was in the hospital with a badly broken leg for three weeks. A few of her friends stopped by but I noticed that all of them felt so uncomfortable that they ended up bolting for the door. Kids seldom just "chat," they talk while playing. After I brought in a few board games and snacks and left them alone, the visits became a success. As soon as my daughter could use a wheelchair, she entertained in the solarium rather than in her hospital room.

Parent

- Keep a diary. Writing may help to keep your thoughts in perspective or it may help vent fears and frustrations. Either way the diary will become fascinating reading for your child in years to come.
- Your children at home may feel left out and even resent their hospitalized sibling. Now is the time to reel in favors. Perhaps family members or neighbors could take your kids on special outings. You might want to have a talk with their teachers as well.

5

School Days

Choosing a Preschool or a Play School

It's not as easy as you may think. Most preschools are private and therefore personal finances will play a part in the choice of school as will location and type of education offered. Some schools place the accent on arts and crafts while others are method schools (Montessori and the Waldorf, for example). In many cases you can read about the philosophy of the program, but keep in mind that not all directors or teachers have the same practical interpretation.

Different schools have different philosophies, so have a long chat with the director and the teacher before you make your decision.

- Spend time sitting in on the classes.
- Watch for eye contact between the teacher and the students.
- Does the teacher greet the children in the morning or does she greet the parents of the children?
- Do the children seem happy and eager?
- Does the teacher know each child by name?
- What are the teacher's qualifications?
- Look around you. The room itself should be bright and airy and the equipment well-kept. The room should also be divided into sections — one space for toys, another for books, a third for art supplies, and so on.
- An overabundance of rules is not a good sign. Children should be able to talk to a pal although yelling must not be allowed. When little children are involved, boundaries should be set but flexible.
- Ask questions: What would happen if my child got hurt? (Which hospital do they use?) What is the ratio between teacher and children? What would happen if my child wet her pants? If I was late in picking up my child, what would the staff do?

One day I got my carpool instructions mixed up. The school called to tell me that my son was waiting. I drove as fast as I could but it still took me twenty minutes to arrive. There, standing inside the door in a very hot waiting area was my three-year-old. He was alone, hot, sweaty, and scared. It's been three years and he is still frightened of being left or not being picked up on time.

Parent

Checking out a Play School for Safety

- The washroom should be on the same level as the classroom. Children who have to "make a run for it" up or down stairs are likely to fall.

- Where are the cleaning supplies kept?
- Are the fire extinguishers kept up-to-date?
- What are the security rules? Are adults allowed to roam the halls without first checking in at the office?
- What is the pick-up and drop-off routine?
- Walk around the playground. Inspect the fencing. Look at the large play equipment. Is it sturdy, well-installed, and well-looked-after? Licensing regulations differ from province to province and state to state; however, health standards are fairly consistent. But ask.

Preparing Your Child

Preschool starts early in your child's life — in many cases right after he is toilet trained. Do all that you can to make those first weeks positive and happy.

- "You will be at play school for two hours" means nothing to the three- year-old who has no concept of time. Relate to her normal schedule. The day before she is to go to school, say "Tomorrow at this time we will be packing up to leave.... Tomorrow at this time you will be having your snack.... Tomorrow at this time I will be returning to your school to pick you up...." Another approach: "Sesame Street is one hour long. I'll be back to pick you up in the time it takes for you to watch Sesame Street two times."
- Several days before play school begins start the school routine. Bed at 7:30, up at 7:00, and so on.
- It's important to attend the school's orientation day. Spend time in the washroom with your child; show him how the doors close and open. Walk through the other classrooms with your child. Open and close the exit doors. If the play school is in a large building (perhaps a school or church basement), talk about boundaries.
- Dress your child for an active day. Pretty patent leather shoes will not help her climb playground ladders. Overalls that

button at the shoulder look adorable but are hard to undo if you are little and need to go to the potty in a hurry. (When in doubt use velcro.)

- Your little one balks at the door and refuses to let go of your hand. Now what? A good teacher will not grab a screaming child and tell you to beat a hasty retreat. Instead you may be asked to sit quietly in the corner while the teacher tries to get your child interested in an activity. The next day you may stay for a shorter period of time. By the third day, and if no one pushes it, your child may be comfortable enough to stay alone. Don't rush the process.
- In some cases you may have no choice but to leave a screaming child. Give him a big hug, verbally reassure him, and exit. For your own sanity you may want to hide out in the hall for a few minutes. Bets are your child will calm down quickly.
- Children worry about their parents. Tell your child exactly what you will be doing while he is at play school. Be precise. "I will go home and work on my computer for two hours. Then I will make the beds and have a cup of tea. I will pick you up when all the other parents pick up their children. Then you and I will go shopping." Be certain to arrive when the other parents do.

Kindergarten and Grade One

Few children enter kindergarten "cold" — most have been in day care or some type of play or cooperative school. However, kindergarten is a step into the real world and every kid knows it.

- If you would like your child to buddy-up with another student to and from school, give the school secretary a call in late August and ask for her help in locating another student who lives nearby.

- Walk the route to and from school with your child several times. Introduce yourself and your child to any crossing guards along the way. Point out block parent homes to your child. Give explicit instructions about shortcuts.
- If there is no orientation day, arrange to meet the teacher with your child in tow at least once before school starts. Introduce yourself and child. Walk around the school with your child and perhaps take a few snapshots. They'll be good fun to look at in years to come and meanwhile your child can study them.
- Talk about school in realistic terms. Your child won't always have a great time, nor will she spend every waking hour knee-deep in artwork.
- Before your child exerts her individuality she must feel accepted by her peers. Within reason, let her dress the part. Youngsters do not like to look radically different from their peers. Consider the lunch box and schoolbag as part of her uniform and let her pick them out.
- Don't give your little one too much liquid in the morning, at least not until he is familiar with the layout of the school. (Wet pants are an embarrassment every child can do without.) Make sure he goes to the bathroom before he leaves for school. And remind him to make a pit stop before boarding the bus or walking home after school.
- Children who are given great amounts of lunch or milk money may become targets for bullies.
- If your child is to eat lunch in the cafeteria, have her practice carrying a loaded tray at home.
- "I have to go dumps" or "I have to go pee-pee" will get belly laughs at school. Teach your child to be excused by saying, "May I go to the washroom (toilet), please?"
- Tuck identification into the schoolbag along with a change of underwear and pants (just in case). But don't label the lunch box or buy a shirt with "Bobby" on the front. The chances are slim but in abduction attempts a child will more readily go with a stranger who knows his name.

- Don't forget to take a picture of your child as she heads out the door.

The Bus

Missing the bus can spell disaster for parents who work outside the home. Prepare for the inevitable.

- Post the number of a cab company by the phone. Keep the money for it in a special envelope.
- Are there other parents in the neighborhood who drive their children to school? Post their numbers as an alternative.
- If your child must stay home because of a missed bus, do not allow television or other fun activities.
- Review bus rules.

Homework

Should your young scholar be given homework? Your child's school or teacher will likely have definite opinions, so ask. Regardless, it's a good idea to set aside an after-dinner or after-school quiet time. If there is homework to be done, fine. If not, a quiet read, without television or telephone interruptions, is a good idea.

After dinner, and after the dishes are washed, we all sit down to different projects. My husband and I may do the bills or read, our three-year-old may color, and the two older kids do their homework. I need this time to relax and since the half hour or so is established, the older kids do not kick up a fuss.

Parent

- No background music or noise during homework or quiet time. (Maybe our parents fell for that "I-can-concentrate-with-Jimmy-Hendrix-playing" routine, but we know better.)

- Make a comfortable area to study in. If there is space, put a desk in the kitchen. Or put pens, pencils, crayons, sharpener, ruler, paper, eraser, scissors, and glue in one box and bring it to the kitchen table. Call it your child's "office box."
- Think twice about sending your child to her room to do homework. If she is also sent to her room for misbehavior, she may look upon homework as punishment.
- Invest in an electric pencil sharpener. No parent need go through life with nicked fingers thanks to sharpening blunt pencils with dull kitchen knives.

Imagine washing windows all day, coming home, and having your mother make you wash windows at night "for practice!" That's how many children view homework.

Teacher

- If homework is assigned by a teacher, parents should not consider themselves responsible for its completion. Help your child but don't nag. If your child doesn't want to do it, so be it. Let him suffer the consequences from the teacher.
- Parents nevertheless should keep on top of things if only to provide various project supplies. (Otherwise, you'll end up scrounging the neighborhood for styrofoam balls at midnight.)
- Provide your kids with a calendar and have them mark off due dates for class projects.
- Keep in touch with your child's teacher.
- If your child is to memorize something and she's having trouble, have her recite it into a recorder.
- Time is of the essence. Between school, the bus rides, hockey, and piano practice, time is also a rare commodity. Be aware of the stresses in your child's life.

- Talk about school projects at the dinner table. If parents think they are important, so will children.

My son started cheating in Grade Two. He was terrified of not getting good marks, of failing. We realized that if we were to change his behavior we'd also have to change our own. We began to accent the "love of learning" for the sake of it. My husband and I stopped putting our attention on marks. We tried to relate what he was learning at school to the world around him. When he did a project on dinosaurs, for example, we took him to the museum. He and his dad did a tour of the municipal dump when he had to write a few paragraphs on cleaning up the environment. He's in Grade Four now and editor of the school paper.

Parent

Good Morning

Getting several children off to school and yourself to work may mean that mornings are hectic. There are ways to make the morning "up-and-at-'em" time pass with fewer frustrations. The obvious ideas are to get organized the night before but here are some less obvious ones.

GETTING UP

- Do a time study. Exactly how long does it take to have a shower, get dressed, have a coffee? Plot out your morning realistically.
- Turn off the AM radio station. That nonstop chatter may only add to the confusion. If you need to hear the weather or traffic report, find an unobtrusive FM station that will provide both. Or use clock radios in the bedroom but maintain radio silence in the kitchen.

- Let the kids have their own alarm clocks and make them responsible for waking themselves up. (It takes time but it's worth it in the long run.) A calendar on the wall will remind them of any early wake-up days.
- Collect funny wake-up songs on a cassette.
- Start the school-night-bedtime/morning-wake-up schedule a week before school starts.

Every morning I got up with my son and husband — got them organized, cooked, found missing socks and tie clips. Inevitably I ended up frustrated and angry. I am not a morning person. A year ago I was ill for three months and my son and husband learned to fend for themselves. The two hummed along like a well-oiled machine. Both are morning people. My husband now actually brings me tea to keep me in bed and out of the way! I love it.

Parent

THE BATHROOM

- Stable step stools by the sink are a must.
- If the washcloth, nailbrush, toothbrush, dental floss, and hairbrush are grouped together, your child is less likely to forget a step.
- Put towels and clothes on easy-to-reach hooks.
- It's impossible to keep a close eye on kids in the bath while you are trying to get dressed. Make bathtime anytime but morning.

MAKING BEDS

- Let your child sleep in a sleeping bag. In the morning she can roll it up into a ball and shove it under her bed. (To keep dry cleaning costs down, fold a sheet in half and stitch it together. Use it as the bag's liner.)

- Opt for a comforter or duvet and forget a top sheet. Making a bed now means tossing up the cover.

It never failed. I'd spend most of the morning yelling answers to questions like "Where are my pink tights?" By the time my girls actually sat down to eat, we were all sniping at each other. Now the rule is "No Yelling". If they want to ask me a question, they have to come down and talk to me. Rather than make the trip they now solve the dilemma themselves.

Parent

Dressing

MAKING IT EASY

Go easy on yourself. If they don't like it, don't buy it because they won't wear it. This immediately minimizes one source of morning stress.

- Mini sets of drawers (a bedside table with shelves plus small baskets will do) are easier to handle than large, heavy drawers. In one drawer put only matched socks, in another only underwear. Open baskets set on shelves work well too.
- All drawers should have "stops" to prevent them from falling out on toes.
- Set aside one drawer or basket for single socks only. The second sock will reappear sooner or later.
- Split your child's closet in half. Hang out-of-season clothes up on top. Stretch a second rod across the closet at your child's height for easy access.
- Hooks, strategically placed behind doors, are obviously easier to use than hangers.

- Children are more likely to put their laundry in the hamper if they have a laundry basket in their room.

GETTING DRESSED

Dawdling children can drive the best of us around the bend! It's tempting to take over the dressing process but be careful — too much interference can create helplessness in children.

- Stand behind your child when buttoning or zipping up a shirt. Let him see the process.
- Teach your child to button from the bottom up.
- Teach your child to sit down when pulling on pants, especially stiff jeans, otherwise child and pants will topple over.
- To take off a pullover tell your child to pull out her arms first and then pull the shirt or sweater over her head.
- Pretend you are dressing a manikin and lay the clothes out as they are supposed to be worn. Or, layer the clothes — underwear on top, then socks, shirt, pants, sweater.
- Choose belt clasps carefully as they are difficult to master. Mark the hole frequently used with a felt pen or sticker.
- If a zipper is sticky run a bar of soap or soft lead pencil over it.
- Buy easy-to-pull-on socks. (Tube socks are not recommended for active sportswear as they do not have a "natural wick action." However, for everyday wear, give yourself a break and buy fifty pairs of identical socks that will fit all of your kids.)
- Labels usually go on the back. Point out this little fact.
- If a button falls off, sew it back on with elastic thread. Buttoning up will now be easier. Or sew the button on with dental floss; it will never break.
- It's easier to tell back-to-front if there is a design on the front.
- Overalls, or pants with bibs attached, are hard to unbutton and can be a nuisance to children in the midst of potty training. Either forget about overalls or replace the shoulder buttons or hooks with velcro.

SHOES

- With a marker make an X on the instep of each shoe. Your child will know that his shoes are on the right feet when the X's kiss.
- If you must buy shoes with laces, lace the shoes and tie knots just before the last two holes. The laces will not slip out easily.
- To teach lacing and tying, use two colors of laces on the same shoe. Your child will see how the laces weave up the shoe. (Substitute red and black licorice strings to make the lessons fun and tasty.)
- Turn a lace-up shoe into a slip-on by threading it with sewing elastic.
- Running shoes should be laced. They will stay on longer and give more support.
- Rub a raw potato over scuffs before polishing. The scuffs should wipe off easily.
- For a fast polish rub shoes with petroleum jelly. (In a pinch hand cream may substitute.)
- A quick squirt of hair spray will keep liquid shoe polish on the shoe longer.
- If you don't want liquid shoe polish to dribble onto the lip of the shoe, coat the rim with clear nail polish. Shoe polish will not stick to the nail polish.
- Put a thin strip of reflective (not fluorescent) tape on the heels of your child's shoes. Not only will this little trick keep him safer at night but it will make the shoes easier to spot in a pile of shoes.
- Scuff up the bottom of leather shoes with sandpaper. Add snippets of a bathtub decal to your toddler's boots to lessen the chance of slipping.

OUTER CLOTHES

Are one-piece snowsuits better than two-piece? It's debatable. One-piece suits tend to keep a child cosier (after all, there are no exposed bits) but two-piece suits tend to fit longer.

- Spray fabric stain protector on woolen coats or clothes that do not directly touch the skin. Spills can now be easily wiped away.
- Zipper tags can be hard to clasp if you are little. Attach a key ring to the zipper tag.
- A child who wears a hat, hood, and scarf may not hear an oncoming car or that all-important honk. One hat and a shell hood that's attached to the jacket is all a child really needs.
- Choose brightly colored snowsuits. Attach strips of reflective tape under the collar (to be flipped up at dusk).
- If you have more than one child, color-code your kids' schoolbags, lunch boxes, and gym bags.
- A large basket placed near the door can collect mittens, hats, scarves. (Buy half a dozen identical mittens at a time.)
- Many kids plus many boots make for a booby-trapped entrance. Keep a bag of colored clothespins in the basket and have the children clip their boots together. (Expect at least one child to pinch himself immediately. Seldom will it happen a second time!)

SCHOOL UNIFORMS

Lucky is the parent whose child wears a uniform to school. True, the initial cost of tunic, blazer, assorted shirts, and gray flannel pants can send you through the roof, but in the long run you'll save money.

- Buy the basics at the end-of-term clothing sale at your child's school. If there is no such sale ask why. (Even the best of schools have them, darling.)
- Use velcro to secure letters or crests to sweaters. Peel them off before washing the sweaters.
- Back the knees of flannel pants before the first wear. Use iron-on patches. Tack the patches with a few well-placed stitches.

SPORTS UNIFORMS

- Designate one bag for each sport. Wash out (better yet teach your child to wash out) the uniform right after a game. Dry and put it back in the bag immediately. (Mixing uniforms with daily wear is deadly.)

- One cup (250 mL) of dishwasher detergent in a few buckets of water often whitens really dirty white uniforms. Soak overnight and then wash in a regular cycle.
- Rub a new baseball mitt with mink oil. Put a baseball in the mitt and close the mitt over the ball with string or elastic bands. Leave for a few days.
- To avoid a case of head lice, either buy your child her own baseball batting helmet or ask the coach to make it a rule that all little leaguers keep their baseball hats on under the helmet.

6

Playtime

Toys

Toys have been called "a child's working tools." What a toy is, or is not, depends on the use it's put to. A small metal car, for example, can "vroom-vroom" all over the house but when it's used to deck baby sister, it's a weapon.

Toys fall into three general categories: basic toys such as blocks of all sorts, balls, and stuffed animals, used by all ages in different ways; educational toys, such as puzzles and games that a child will learn from and eventually grow out of; novelty toys, such as wind-up or "watch and see" toys that have minimum value — other than monetary, of course!

Generally speaking, an educational toy stretches a child's imagination and understanding of himself. It demands that a child ask, "What can I do with this?" It empowers the child and makes her feel good about herself.

Novelty toys can be fun but your toy-spending money should go first on the basic toys rather than the highly priced novelty toys (which in reality tend to attract adults more than kids anyway).

- Match toys to a child's age and interests. An infant under three months needs visual stimulation. Paper plates decorated with big faces and pictures of faces cut out from magazines and backed with cardboard qualify as toys. (Happy faces are perennial favorites.)
- Crib mobiles should face downward so baby can see the mobile elements.
- Infant and baby toys should stimulate motor, perceptual and visual skills.
- Crib toys should be soft. If baby rolls over on them even the most well-designed rigid toy will wake baby up.
- Buy multi-colored socks, or socks designed with colored toes. Or, put a blue sock on one foot and a red sock on the other. It's a hoot to look at baby's face as she watches her socks wiggle and dance.

Toy Safety

- Crib mobiles have been known to fall into cribs. Each part of the mobile should be too big to fit into your baby's mouth — that is, no smaller than her closed fist. Remove the mobile as soon as she begins to push herself up on her arms, typically between five and six months. Replace the mobile with a colorful kite or a poster stuck to the ceiling.
- Forget about crib toys that span the width of the crib. They have been known to cause choking and strangulation if not removed before a baby can push himself up.

- Never, ever, give an infant a balloon. The pop could damage her ears and balloon bits could be swallowed and cause suffocation.
- Never buy handmade toys for children under three at a church jumble sale or country fair. If the toy is stuffed you have no way of knowing just what's inside. Homemade wooden toys that are glued have a way of becoming unglued.
- If the string on your child's pull toy keeps getting tangled, run it through a bit of cut-up garden hose. Hold the top of the string in place with a block.
- With stuffed toys opt for embroidered eyes rather than button eyes.
- Long bunny ears, elephant noses, or stringy tails can be chewed. A baby may accidentally stuff one down her throat.
- Listen to the toy. Could it cause hearing damage to a child?

Toy Storage

- The lids on toy boxes crush little fingers. Opt instead for soft, colorful laundry baskets. (An open shelf in your child's room can also be designed to accommodate toys.)
- To keep little toys from roaming about on their own, store them in plastic yogurt cups glued to a tray.
- A colorful rope plus multicolored clothes pegs run across one wall of your child's room will show off all of her artwork.
- Stuffed creatures might be housed in the pockets of a plastic shoe keeper.
- What to do with your six-year-old's tiny toys when you have an active eighteen-month-old who noshes everything in sight? Make a toy closet. Remove the clothes (use the top of the closet for seasonal clothes storage) and insert shelves in the lower half. Place toys on the shelves. When the closet is open, your older child may play to her heart's delight. Install a hook-and-eye catch out of both children's reach on the outside of the closet door to prevent unsupervised play.
- Keep your older child's small toys in plastic kitchen baskets. The baskets can be brought out when your toddler is napping.

- If both children must share a room, make a play space for your older child in another part of the house.

Keeping Things Tidy

- Make a "play cloth." Cut a large circle out of an old sheet. Run a cord through a seam around the outer edge. Spread out, it forms a big circle to play with Zacks or Lego on. Cleanup is a pull of the cord.

My five-year-old's room was a disaster area. No matter what I said my son would not clean up after himself. It finally dawned on me that I had never taught him how to clean up. I sat in his room with him and one by one we found a "place" for each toy. Cleanup wasn't nearly so difficult once he had learned how.

Parent

- Give individual toys a place to live. Mark their spots with pictures of the toys (cut them out of magazines and catalogues.)
- Big trucks should always go on the bottom shelf to prevent them from falling on little toes.
- Divide the mess into areas (floor, bed, desktop) and have your child clean up one area at a time.
- The best time to tidy up is after playtime, or so most adults think. But since tidy-up means the end of playtime, most children will resist. Tidy up halfway through playtime. Pick up the last of the toys yourself.
- Play a marching tune during tidy-up time.
- Use a timer and see how fast the children can put all the toys back.
- Play "copycat" — you put away a toy, then child puts away a toy.

- No one likes to tidy up alone. Help out.
- Wrap an apron with large pockets around your child and tell her to go through the house and fill the pockets with all the toys she can find.
- Give your child a basket and tell him to go shopping for toys all around the house.
- Clean toys by wiping them with a cloth dipped in water and baking soda or toss them into a bag containing baking soda.

For more information on toys:
The Canadian Toy Testing Council (CTTC) produces *The Toy Report*, an in-depth child-tested survey of toys, every year before Christmas. These books are sold on store shelves or can be ordered by writing: CTTC, 881 Lady Ellen Place, Ottawa, Ontario K1Z 5L3. Phone: (613) 729-7101.

The Canadian Association of Toy Libraries and Parent-Child Resources Centres (TLRC — Canada). To find out about a toy lending library in your area or how to start a library, contact: TLRC, 205-120 Holland Avenue, Ottawa, Ontario K1Y 0X6. Phone: (613) 728-3307.

Outside Play

- Battery-operated toys become a hazard when they take off down the driveway by themselves. Little children have been known to follow them — right into traffic.
- Tall flags should be hoisted, and secured, onto low-riding trikes and bikes. Without the flag, the riding child may not be spotted by a driver backing out of a driveway.
- Opt for rubber rather than plastic wheels on any riding toy. Plastic wheels with seams tend to split.
- Make an outside toy storage area.
- Sandboxes are used by toddlers and six-year-olds alike. Rake the sand often and keep it covered at night to prevent the local tomcat from using it as a litter box.

- If you want to design your own backyard playground, I recommend *Home Playgrounds: The Harrowsmith Guide to Building Backyard Play Structures*, Merilyn Mohr, Camden House.

Crafty Ideas

If you actually *like* kneading playdough, if you enjoy the challenge of building a working volcano, if you positively revel in the idea of sinking calf-deep in reams of papier-maché, then "pass" on this section. This is for those of us who consider crafts a necessary, but evil, part of parenthood.

"Survival" Recipes: The Bare Minimum

PLAYDOUGH
3 cups (750 mL) flour
1 1/2 cups (375 mL) salt
2 tablespoons (30 mL) cream of tartar
3 cups (750 mL) water
1 tablespoon (15 mL) oil (optional)

Mix wet ingredients separately from dry ingredients. Blend together. Divide into portions and add a different shade of food coloring to each. Stir each portion over low heat until a ball is formed. Let cool, and store in airtight container in the fridge.

Safety Note: It sounds like a fun idea to make edible playdough (usually made with a peanut butter concoction) but it's not a good idea to get children into the habit of eating playdough.

SALT DOUGH
2 cups (500 mL) flour
1 cup (250 mL) water
1 cup (250 mL) salt

Blend ingredients and knead.

Note: To make hanging ornaments, break salt dough into cookie-sized rounds and design faces. Use a garlic press to make spaghetti-like hair. Bake at 3OO° F (150° C) until hard. Then paint. To turn the faces into fridge magnets, pop into a craft store and buy magnetic tape by the inch.

FINGER PAINT
1/4 cup (50 mL) laundry starch
2 drops food coloring or natural alternative

Mix and use on thick paper. Try crumbling bits of powdered paint into the mixture for extra texture and color.
Another idea: Put several large glops of shaving cream on tinfoil or shelf paper. Add a different color of food coloring to each glop. Stir.

Painting and Coloring

- Mix a few drops of liquid dishwasher soap with tempera paint. The paint should wash out easily. Otherwise, tempera paint (and crayon stains) can be removed with baking soda.
- Cupcake tins make great little containers for glues and paints.
- Cut a large kitchen sponge into several small sponges. Pour paint into little trays. Your child can use them to roll or smear on the paint.
- To make a painting tray take a large piece of foam rubber or sponge and cut out holes the size of yogurt containers. Fill the yogurt cups with paint and insert into the openings.
- Store felt pens in a glass jar with a tight lid. If the pens are in the process of drying out, rejuvenate them with a ten-minute soak in lukewarm water.
- To make a painting smock, turn a plastic garbage bag upside down and cut head and arm holes in the appropriate places (recommended for children over the age of five). Or cut the

sleeves and collar off an old plastic raincoat and put it on the child backwards.

- Take one new box of crayons. Wrap each crayon in the middle with a strip of masking tape. The crayons will now be very hard to snap into two.
- Sharpen a crayon by dipping the tip in hot water or placing it in the sun. Roll the tip between your fingers to form a point.
- To make a cleanable painting area in your home, ask for old vinyl samples at a flooring store. Cut out an appropriate size as a mat for the floor. Another mat may be tacked onto a light-weight board and used as a table-top.
- Children under three are still tempted to eat paints and munch on felt pens. Supervise carefully. Avoid felt pens and paints that smell like food — for example, purple pens that smell like grapes, red pens that smell like cherries. They tend to confuse a child who is trying to learn about what is poisonous and what is not.

Safety Note: Printed on the packages of many art supplies designed for children is the word "nontoxic." Toxicity levels as a rule refer to adult susceptibility. What may be borderline toxic to an adult may be very toxic to a child. For a list of commercially marketed art materials that are safe write to: The Art and Craft Materials Institute Inc., 1715 Boylston Street, Boston, MA 02116, U.S.A.

Scissors and Cutting Out

- Blunt scissors are frustrating and can cause accidents. Give your child round-tipped scissors that are sharp enough to cut paper. Teach her how to walk with them and hand them to other people.
- To keep scissors sharp use them to cut up medium-grade sandpaper.
- Collages are the easiest projects to do with children. Take cardboard grocery boxes or a laundry hamper and toss in

collectibles as you find them — swatches of material, cardboard, bits of yarn, wrapping paper, egg cartons, buttons, feathers, sequins, macaroni, greeting cards. Small beads and baubles may be collected in an egg carton. In a month or so you'll have a great collection. Invite a few kids over, dole out the bristol board and glue, and wait for spectacular results.

Where to Find Art Supplies

As well as toy stores and art supply stores there are other sources for art materials.

- At the butcher shop brown-paper rolls can be bought in bulk and mounted on a doweling rod directly on the wall.
- A printer's shop often has small mountains of paper to discard or may offer bulk newsprint at a discount.
- Drop by a wallpaper outlet and ask for their old, soon-to-be-discarded wallpaper books. The samples can be used to wallpaper a dolls' house, to create greeting cards or collages, or to make a scrapbook.

Displaying Your Child's Art

My son did a beautiful drawing of our home. I took it in and had it professionally framed for my husband's office. We thought this would encourage him to keep up his drawing. Instead, it seemed to overwhelm him. Years later he said he had stopped drawing because he thought he could never do a picture as well as the one I had framed.

Parent

- String a string across the wall of your child's room or window and, with the help of colored clothes pegs, display your child's art. Change the pieces often.

Gifts for Kids to Make

- Make a collection of finger puppets for a little brother or sister. Take an old glove and chop off the fingers. Pretend that each finger is a member of the family and decorate accordingly.
- Most craft supply stores carry barrette clips and an assortment of pins. Buy a few packets and let your child make all sorts of jewelry for the relatives. Bells, buttons, bows, clay, and Fimo (a commercial product found in art supply stores) can be used to produce these wearable objets d'art.
- Collect a small mountain of odd crayon bits. Remove the paper, place on tinfoil, and lay out in the sun. When melted roll together to make one giant crayon. Put in the fridge. This giant crayon plus a giant coloring book makes a great gift for a sick friend.
- Put a small dish in the bathroom and have the family toss in soap that is too small to handle. When you have enough scraps, gently melt them in the sun. Have your child roll the pieces into small balls, dry, and place in a little basket for a gift for the teacher.
- To make bubble bath put soap bits in a squishy, liquid detergent bottle. Add water and let sit for a few days. Decorate the bottle.
- Make a picture window for a bed-bound friend. Help your child grate up a few old crayons. Sandwich the bits between two sheets of wax paper. Cover with a page of newspaper and iron until the wax crayons have melted into an interesting blur. Let dry or harden. Trim into any any shape and poke a hole in the top for a string.
- Take a photo of your child doing one activity each month. For instance: September — going off to school; October — dressing up for Halloween; November — rehearsing for the school play; December — opening gifts; January — skating; and so on. Collect the pictures taken over a twelve-month period. Enlarge them. Attach a corresponding calender month to each picture and give Grandpa a very personal

calendar. A simpler version: Have your child make twelve drawings — one for each month.

- Make a silhouette of your child's face (pin paper onto the wall, have your child sit sideways, shine a light on your child, and trace her shadow). Frame your creation for a relative.
- Help your child make a tape of a song or story to send to a sick friend.

Activities

Keep in mind that the best activities are the ones children have designed for themselves. You might still want to prepare a few projects just in case.

Outdoor Activities for Cold Weather

- If it's cold outside (late fall or early spring), give the kids all your ice-cube trays and let them make mini-ice-castles out of the blocks. Make sure that they know they should not lick the ice cubes. Let them take a few choice toys outside too.
- Send your child out into the cold with a bag to collect things to decorate with — pinecones, feathers, evergreen branches. Have paper and paint waiting for her return.
- Sandboxes are as much fun in the fall and spring as they are in the summer. Think twice before covering them up too early.

Outdoor Activities for Warm Weather

- Two buckets of water and two short-handled paintbrushes will keep two toddlers happy for the longest time (about ten minutes). Ask them to paint the house/car/driveway.
- Giant sticks of chalk can be used to decorate the sidewalk.
- Have the kids collect rocks. Spread out some plastic sheeting (the old cover from the picnic table works well here) on the lawn and paint the rocks with water-based paint. Use the rocks to decorate the garden or walkway.

- Collect your old, rinsed-out bleach bottles for an outdoor game of bowling.

Safety Note: Mad dogs, Englishmen, and children go out in the midday sun, and while the former may burn themselves to a crisp, children need sunscreen protection. Parts of their bodies that are regularly missed in a sunscreen dip are under the chin, back of the neck, under the T-shirt (loose weave cotton shirts do not offer substantial protection from the sun), feet and backs of the hands. Of course the entire body is often missed if your child can't stand to be smeared with goop. Look for the latest in sunscreen protection. For example, waterproof sunscreen pads that can be wiped on might be an alternative. Whatever your preferred product, your child will need lots of it. To get an idea of how much, fill your child's cupped hand to the brim with the cream. That is how much cream he will need.

How Does Your Garden Grow?

The garden can teach children about the life cycle, bugs, and responsibility. For example, plants draw moisture from their roots. To make a point, chop off the end of a celery stick and dunk it into a glass of water and red food dye. The leaves on the celery stick will turn color in thirty to forty-five minutes.

Give your child a portion of the garden and suggest she start her own business. She will need a lot of help the first year but after that she might be the one helping you. If there is no space available use window boxes and flower pots.

A trip to a local garden center and a conversation with a real gardener will spur on her interest. So will the tools of the trade. A beginner's set of gardening tools need not cost more than $10.00 or so, providing you already have the basic shovels and such. It is important, however, that your child have her own set of tools.

The chance of your child losing interest is excellent — after all, plants do not grow immediately. In some cases your child may just be too young, in other cases she might just get bored. Waylay the boredom by germinating the seedlings indoors or by buying sprouts at a garden center.

Collect seed books during the winter and let her pick the plants to grow. She may want to grow flowers, in which case she may turn them into a potpourri or bunch them together and sell them at the base of the driveway. (An adult should oversee such sales.)

Herb gardens are another easy-to-grow alternative. Bottled in little jars and collected in a basket, herbs make ideal gifts.

Don't discount a vegetable garden. There is nothing as tasty as corn grown "all by myself." Vegetables too can be sold to the neighbors.

Indoor Activities for Rainy Days

- Comic books cost a fortune. Stack and save the weekend comics and bring them out on a rainy day. (Some moms prefer to save them for sick days.)
- Make a snow jar. Take a small jar with a screw-on lid. Glue a small figure (a plastic finger-sized doll or house) to the inside lid. Add mini-squares of tinfoil to the jar. Fill with water. Screw lid on tightly. Shake and tip upside down.
- Take a giant office calendar. Give your children pennies and challenge them to flick the pennies so that they land on a specific date.
- Keep empty gift boxes and let your child make box sculptures. She may glue all the boxes together, paint, and decorate them or she may fill up one box with a new creation.
- Collect a box of crafty things and pull it out when you are at your wit's end. Include popsicle sticks, cast-off ribbons and bows, old egg cartons, markers and crayons, glue and sheets

of paper. (See the section on "Crafty Ideas" earlier in this chapter for lots of ideas on what to do with all these things.)

And finally, here's an idea for rainy days in the summertime. Draw up a summertime calendar (make one if you must) and plan an activity for each day. Scale the activities according to age and development. Here are some examples for children aged six to eight. Monday: Write out as many words as you can that end with the letters "al." Tuesday: Take one page from an old newspaper and circle all the words that begin with the letter "c." Wednesday: Go to the library and find out how a "rebus" works. Thursday: Take the atlas and plot a trip across Europe. Friday: Sketch a monarch butterfly.

THE WRITTEN WORD

Introducing books to your children is not only the gift of a lifetime but while they are immersed in books the noise level of your home will plummet. However, in a world of mega-toy-advertising, children may need a little, or a lot, of gentle persuasion to see books from our point of view.

- Start "reading" to your baby soon after birth. (What the heck — it's fun.) Babies love rhymes. At this young age the focus is on the sounds rather than on the words.
- Toddlers enjoy participation books with flip-up pages. *I Can Roar* by Frank Ask, (Kids Can Press) and *Where's Spot?* by Eric Hill (Putnam) are two examples. *Note*: Before you give your child flip-up books, reinforce the "flaps" on each page with clear tape. Children need to be taught how to treat books gently.
- Most cloth books, designed for toddlers, make good dishrags and that's about all. The words are usually illegible, the "pages" impossible to turn, and no one has ever been known to actually "read" one.
- Plastic books and books that one must blow up (presumably with air) are not books at all. They are toys with words written on them.

- If you don't always have time to read to your child, tape a book. Simply run a tape while you are reading to your child and let her play it back another night. (This idea is especially good if you travel a lot.)
- While there are no absolute rules here, small children like to read about the real world — animals, bugs, their own bodies, planes, trains and all things that move. Typically, children over six become more interested in the supernatural — fairies, tall tales, things scary and dreamy.
- Reading comprehension and word memorization should not be confused but it's fun to teach little ones to recognize a few key words such as "exit" and "stop." Try labeling some of the things in your home. Write out words on cardboard strips (table, chair, door, Dad) and pin or tape them up. Make a game of sticking them back in their correct places.
- Some books truly are "disposable" and need not be well made. Comic books, coloring books, joke books, or any softcover books destined for the backseat of the car fit into this category. Books designed to be read and reread, thumbed through, and petted must be sturdy. Examine the binding, the back and front cover, the page quality.

Try not to force your taste in books on children. Your old childhood favorites may never be of interest to your children. Remember that you were never the age that your children are now. Today's child has different problems to deal with and she may want books that identify, recognize, or deal with her world.

Many children have difficulty reading. Parents and teachers often react (read "overreact") by enrolling the child in extra reading classes. Some librarians respond by piling the kids with books, the attitude being, "Kids can use them to block up a window for all we care."

Easy-does-it. We all learn at our own pace. Some four-year-olds can "read", (although comprehension may be limited) while other kids might not be ready to read until they are well into elementary school. Given an accepting atmosphere, these children will catch up in no time. To push the issue and "make" a child read is counter productive; not only may a child feel stupid, but he may resent and blame books for his problems.

"Setting the right atmosphere" means creating an environment that includes books.

- If you have pushed specific books at your child in the past, relinquish the reins to a more neutral person. Call up a children's bookstore, for example, and have an honest chat with the owner or a recommended salesperson about new books. (Many of the salespeople in specialty bookstores are very well informed, some are not. Shop around.) Try making "an appointment" of sorts with the salesperson and your child. Give them a budget and leave the two alone. *Note*: A good librarian will provide your child with the same service described above.
- Get your child a library card and show her "all the services". (In many libraries one can borrow records, movies, and all sorts of things.)
- Read everything with your child – posters, signs, menus (always insist that your child receive his or her own menu). Show children how the written word is used on the street and in everyday life.
- Give your reluctant reader easy-to-read books (without being condescending). The idea is to enjoy the read, not struggle through every page.
- Take out a subscription, in your child's name, to a magazine on a topic that interests her.
- "Read" newspaper comics together. Or follow up a hockey game with a perusal through the sports section of the newspaper.
- Leave notes on the fridge and jokes in their lunch boxes.
- Continue to read to children long after they can actually read to themselves. The physical closeness of a good read between adult and child will be remembered along with the story.

- A hockey lover who has never read a biography might be willing to read a book about his favorite player. A child who likes to garden but hates to read might be enticed by a book on gardening. Likewise, a child who has recently received a new puppy might be willing to read a book on dog training.
- Don't forget to buy joke books!
- Buy your would-be-chef a cookbook.
- If your child has a rigid bedtime, consider giving this option: "Bedtime is at 8:00 but you may read until 8:30." (Who cares if they read into the night. Sleep can be an overrated use of time.)
- Give your child two allowances. (In reality you may be breaking one allowance into two parts.) One part is for optional spending; the second part must go on books or be returned to you.
- Take your child to a play or movie and buy "the book" later on. (Surprise! Many kids will prefer the book to the play/movie.)

My parents loved books and magazines. They were everywhere — on dozens of shelves, in the bathroom, stacked in the hall, crammed under the stairs. I can't ever remember a meal without a bunch of books precariously balanced on the corner of the table. At my friend's house, however, books were like figurines — for show only. I remember reaching for one and having my hand slapped. I was told that children would only 'dirty' the pages. Needless to say, my friend did not read much.

Adult

- Create a "reading space" in your child's room — a light and a big pillow beside the bookshelves will do it.
- Dig out that old typewriter and let your child play with it.

The best way to encourage reading is to read yourself and show your child how much you enjoy books. Share, read passages out loud, go to books for instructions, entertainment and ideas. And if the book your child has chosen (*Tom Sawyer, The Merchant of Venice*) does not reflect your values, please don't ban the book. Talk about values. Compare the written thoughts with present-day feelings.

Books have hundreds of uses and only one is propping up a chair leg.

For more on children's literature:

The Children's Literature Service, National Library of Canada, provides yearly lists of recommended reading for children at no cost. Address: 395 Wellington Street, Ottawa, Ontario K1A 0N4. Phone: (613) 996-2300 or 996-7774.

The Canadian Children's Book Centre is a nonprofit resource center that promotes Canadian children's authors and illustrators. Membership fee is $20.00. Address: 229 College Street, 5th Floor, Toronto, Ontario M5T 1R4.

Children's Book Club, Junior Literacy Guild, Membership Secretary, Customer Service Center, 501 Franklin Avenue, Garden City, NY 11530, U.S.A.
Note: Write for membership guidelines.

MUSIC

It's all around us so don't relegate music to the stereo or to one piano lesson a week.

- Play tapes and records while your child is painting or playing with toys.
- Attend a music class before enrolling your child. Watch the students, reactions to the teacher and the class. Don't always judge a class by how the children look when they leave. Most teachers plan a special event for the last five minutes.
- Make musical instruments with your child. Bottle caps pierced with a nail and strung on a cord make an interesting sound. Fill glass bottles with different levels of water,

provide your child with a short-handled wooden spoon and listen to her make a tune. Make maracas by putting beans in a jar. Screw the lid on extra tight.

- Let your child rummage through the pots and pans. Presto, a kitchen band!
- Collect inexpensive musical instruments from different countries.
- Play all sorts of records and tapes — classical to western to hard rock.
- Spin a disk, give your child a baton, and let her "conduct" a concert.
- Play music, classical is best, and ask your child what he "sees." Does the music remind him of soldiers marching? Fairies dancing? Horses runnning?
- Give your child her own tape deck if finances allow. Careful with earphones and headsets. She may damage her eardrums if the volume is turned up too loud.

7

Time Out: Excursions

Spur-of-the-moment excursions are fun but when children are involved, the planning can be as exciting as the actual event.

- Bring a change of clothes for your youngsters. Excessive excitement causes accidents. On top of that, many rides and activities in amusement parks involve getting soaking wet. (You may want to bring along a change of clothes for yourself as well.)
- Carry no-salt snacks, a damp washcloth in a plastic bag, and a fold-up tote to collect cast-off sweaters and hats.
- Check the weather but think twice about cancelling just because of rain. A rainy walk through the zoo can be a wonderful experience.

- Lunch should be more than feeding time — it should be a rest break. Bring along a book (if you are at the zoo you might carry a book on animals) and let your child peruse it while resting under a tree.
- Don't forget your camera.

We welcome city kids out on our farm during the summer. It amazes me, however, that so many parents have the idea that farms are safe places. I think it goes back to the old idea that "farm life" is synonymous with "simple life." Playing around a working farm is as dangerous as playing near a busy city street.

Farm Owner

Amusement Parks

Won the lottery have you? Well, why not go to an amusement park?

- Given a choice go at night (or as soon as the daily admission fee lowers). Late evenings and nights are magical times for children. The sky might be lit up with fireworks, bands play, teenagers kiss (a favorite exhibition for six- year-olds). The rides are not as crowded and the weather is cool and breezy. Call first and ask about specific rides. Many kiddie rides close long before the park does.
- Feed the children before you go, even if you plan to eat out!
- As soon as you enter the park, turn left. Crowds habitually turn right.
- Attend the most popular display, often at the front of the park, on your way out. It will then be as near to empty as you can get.
- If events are run by the hour (films, hands-on demonstrations, and such), attend the one closest to dinnertime. If, for

example, films run at 2:00, 3:00, 4:00, and 5:00, chances are the 5:00 show will be the least crowded.

- If the park is educational beware of The School Trip. Typically, school buses pick the kids up at 9:00 and deliver them to the science center/museum/exhibition around 10:00. Plan to arrive either very early or very late. (Remember, school trips are carried on by day camps in the summer. There is no reprieve!)

Museum and Gallery Hopping

The object of first trips to the museum should be to familiarize your children with the atmosphere — make them comfortable. Constant shushing will get the opposite reaction.

- Some museums prohibit children from riding in backpacks. (Parents have been known to unwittingly whack an exhibit with the pack. Likewise little arms have long reaches.) To protect floors other museums deter parents from using strollers. Call in advance.
- Ask, in advance, about special programs or kiddie tours. Many galleries have taken it upon themselves to welcome the next generation of art supporters in special ways.
- Young children love, indeed need, to touch objects. Be warned. If the museum is a hands-off one, insist that hands be kept in pockets. Explain the museum rules explicitly.

I know the guard was only doing his job, but when he boomed out "Hands off!" just as my son was reaching up to pet a stone horse, well, that was the end of our first museum visit. My five-year-old was so frightened and embarrassed that he wouldn't go near a museum, or anyone dressed in a uniform, until he was seven.

Parent

- Make it fun. Stop in at the gift shop and pick up some postcards. Now try to find the matching painting.
- The attention span of your little one is limited. The visit should take no more than one hour.
- Focus your attention on your child and save personal viewing for another day.

My three year old ignored the displays but examined each air duct thoroughly.

Parent

- Concentrate on one section of the museum rather than rushing through the entire place. Let the children set the pace.
- Bring along a pair of small binoculars or a magnifying glass for close inspections of fossils.
- Talk about the pictures in a way that would interest your child. For example, young children like to look at other young children. Talk about the children in the paintings: Do they look happy? Do they look comfortable in those old-fashioned clothes? How old are they?
- Talk about the way the work makes you feel. Some modern work might make you giggle. Dark colors may feel spooky, light colors happy.
- Children over six who are into all things spooky might like to haunt an Egyptian exhibit.
- Kids over nine may wish to peruse the gallery by themselves.
- Take an audio tour. As a rule kids love headsets. Rent one if such things are available.
- Young children may prefer three-dimensional objects, such as sculptures, to paintings.

- Children's museums have special appeal, not only because they are geared toward children but because they often have exhibitors displaying their crafts and talents — a glass blower may be blowing glass, a weaver weaving cloth.
- The more familiar children are with art, the more they will enjoy the occasional outing. Take them to the gallery shop and have them pick out posters for their rooms.
- At the end of the visit plan a little physical exercise — a run in the park perhaps.
- "No food or beverages allowed" is the order of the day. Nevertheless you may need a few uppers to waylay the hunger monster. Stash a few jelly beans or whatever in your purse.
- "My kid can paint as well as that guy." A familiar statement and one that may lead children to conclusions that are not their own. The opinions of parents, teachers — all adults — are uncalled-for in this situation. Maybe your child feels that he could indeed paint as well as one particular artist. Inspiration should not be ignored. Once home let your little Picasso loose!

There are some terrific books out for kids that may prepare them for the adventure or may reinforce their memories. However, a good art book should be interesting whether your child is to attend the gallery or not.

- The Art Gallery of Ontario (AGO), for example, provides kids with *The Amazing Clue Book* or *Looking Together* — books filled with riddles and games that put fun into viewing works of art.
- *Discover Mysteries of the Past and Present* by Katherine Grier, Kids Can Press, a Royal Ontario Museum book. It will introduce your child to museums.
- *Meet Edgar Degas* by Anne Newlands, Kids Can Press, National Gallery of Canada. This is a book about an individual artist.

The Movies

- Yikes, it's dark in here! Seldom are children prepared for lights out. Warn them in advance.
- Watch out for those previews. An advertisement for a horror or action film can scare the pants off little ones. If need be, claim your seats and wait out in the lobby until the feature begins.
- Save the rent money — bring juice and your own popcorn in small disposable bags. (Don't make a big production out of it. Most movie-house managers will not appreciate the loss of income.)
- Bring sweaters.
- A booster seat may give your child that extra lift she needs to see over the giant in front of her.
- Take your child to the washroom before sitting down and expect to make at least two return visits during the movie. You'll need an extra adult if you have two children because you shouldn't leave one child unattended in the theater, nor should you let your little one go to the washroom alone.
- Cut out the newspaper ad and keep the ticket stub for your child's diary or scrapbook.
- Your child may enjoy making her own movie poster.

Eating Out

It's good to expose children to fine dining but be realistic. Convincing your child to "just try" escargots is an exercise in futility. Stick to family restaurants during the first five or so years.

- Feed small children before you go out. This sounds redundant but your child will behave better, you'll feel less guilty about him not eating, and everyone will be happier.
- Do not automatically order from the kiddie menu. The selection is limited and you may get a better deal elsewhere

on the menu. Check out the appetizers or get an extra plate and pass food around the table.

- Bring along clothes pegs to hold a napkin in place.
- Stash a juice box in your purse. Restaurant food never comes fast enough.
- Bring along crayons and a coloring book or anything portable that will entertain your child during the time it takes for the food to arrive.
- Restaurants that offer a salad bar are particularly handy. Fill your child up on raw veggies and use the salad dressing as dip.
- Order bread the moment you sit down.
- Get rid of that mustard and ketchup bottle — fast!
- Do not allow your child to run through the restaurant. Not only will he learn bad behavior but a server might spill coffee on him — accidentally, of course.

There are some who might jump down my throat for this, but we have always offered our picky eaters a quarter for trying something new. The result? My four-year-old begged to try Caesar salad and my eight-year-old wanted a new video game so badly that he sampled everything offered, including sushi!

Parent

- Rather than run the risk of wasting a whole meal, have your child order a favorite food and allow her to taste test from your plate.
- Return to the restaurant that treats your family like humans. The more they get to know you, the better the service will become.

Shopping

- Never leave your child alone in a shopping cart. According to the United States Consumer Product Safety Commission, these four-wheeled monsters are responsible for 13,000 accidents annually. Use a harness.
- Children have been known to sup directly from store shelves. Not a great problem if the food your child pinches is the odd grape, but it's a major problem if your child chug-a-lugs cleaning liquids. Watch your child closely and do not allow in-store snacking.

I give my fourteen-month-old a brown paper bag filled with her soft toys to unpack while I am putting away our own groceries.

Parent

- Tie (with a very short string) a small toy to the handle of the cart.
- Keep the trip short. Dragging a toddler around for more than an hour may constitute cruel and unusual punishment — at least from your child's point of view.
- Remind your child about the shopping rules on the way.
- Plan a "kid-stop" — perhaps twenty minutes at a street-side park or if the "I wants" are contained, a breeze through a toy store.
- Discuss the price of things with your three-year-old.
- Give your child a handful of labels (peeled from discarded tins) and let her search out identical labels on the shelves. Coupons with the picture of the products could substitute.
- Many stores offer food sampling on weekends and busy evenings (Thursday and Friday nights). Unless your child has food allergies don't turn up your nose at them. It's

surprising what children will try. My own son discovered a preference for blue cheese, thanks to an in-store cheese tray.

- If your child is over seven encourage him to plan a meal. Shop together for that meal.
- Keep an old umbrella stroller in your trunk for those quick stops with baby.

It's a game we play. Once home from food-shopping my four-year-old sorts the groceries. All the poisonous things (cleaning liquids, etc.) are put at one end of the table and all the edible food is placed at the other end. Once he thought a liquid whitener was a bottle of milk and another time he thought a floor cleaner was a bottle of lemon juice because there was a picture of lemon on the label. Our game has made him mark the differences between edible and poisonous items.

Parent

- A walking harness may get silly comments from passers-by (all from people who do not have children) but it offers more freedom to a child than a stroller.
- Escalators and strollers do not mix. Take an elevator. Show toddlers how to get on and off an escalator. As soon as they are ready, show children how to stop an escalator in an emergency — by pushing the red button at the top or bottom of the escalator.

The "I wants" can ruin your outing.

- Decide on a treat before you enter the store.
- Tell your child in advance how you feel about the "I wants." For example, "I get upset when you demand so many things. Junk food is not good for you." Or "I have not budgeted for toys today."

- Be sure your child understands the consequences of the "I wants". Try "Next time you will have to stay with the baby-sitter."
- Read the shopping list to your child in advance.
- Decide, in advance, which treat is acceptable.
- When food shopping, allow your child to pick out the cereal, having been given the choice of two brands, of course.
- Feed your child before leaving the house or bring a suitable snack.
- Be consistent and firm.
- Sometimes children just can't help themselves! Make a code. If the "I wants" rear their ugly heads, pull on your ear, wrinkle your nose. Such a reminder may banish those nasty demands.
- Every child develops a case of the "I wants." You are not alone!

Of course, you don't always have to do your shopping in malls or stores. Send for mail-order catalogues and choose toys, clothes, and gifts from them.

8

Holidays

Halloween

Should your child be allowed to continue that age-old tradition — trick-or-treating door to door? The answer has more to do with the amount of traffic in your area and your child's street awareness than the much media-touted fear of spiked fruit and candy. Plainly, the major threat to a child's well-being on Halloween is from cars. If you live in a high-traffic area you might do better to have a dress-up party for your children and their friends, so they will have all the fun of wearing costumes and none of the problems of wandering about the streets.

Costumes

- Never make costumes out of bulky cardboard boxes. Such costumes cannot be made flameproof, they are cumbersome, do not allow for a quick exit, and are generally a pain.
- Homemade costumes should not be made with paper or cardboard. Cotton, rayon, linen, acrylic, and acetate are easy to ignite and hard to extinguish.
- Flameproof costumes by dipping fabric into a concoction of: 2 quarts (2 L) warm water, 7 ounces (200 mL) borax, and 3 ounces (85 mL) boric acid. Let the material dry and then iron it. Repeat if costume is washed.
- Very young children may not want to dress up. Don't argue. Suggest big brother's baseball shirt or Dad's work shirt.
- A child's sleeper is by law flame-resistant and makes an excellent base for a costume. A red sleeper may become a devil, a white sleeper a bunny, a green sleeper a Martian, a yellow sleeper a canary.
- Use a sweat suit, complete with hood, as a costume base for older kids. A gray sweat suit may become an elephant (add ears, trunk, and tail), a pink sweat suit may be a base for a princess, a green suit the Green Hornet, a black suit Batman, and so on.
- Running shoes only. Floppy feet or ill-fitting shoes are a hazard and a pain.

Our children have a huge box of old clothes that we add to throughout the year. Come Halloween the kids ransack the box and create their own, very individual, costumes. One year my son was two creatures, half dog/half cat. My kids' imaginations soar and I have minimal expense and fuss.

Parent

- Make a glowing skeleton by dressing your child entirely in black. Now add strips of reflective (not fluorescent) tape and first-aid tape in the shape of ribs and bones. Add a white face.
- Masks slip down and block vision. Consider face makeup. You can make homemade whiteface with: 2 tablespoons (30 mL) cornstarch and 1 tablespoon (15 mL) solid shortening or with 3 tablespoons (45 mL) white shortening (cold cream works too) and 3 tablespoons (45 mL) baby powder or cornstarch. To add color mix in the preferred food coloring. To add spooky shadows add unsweetened cocoa powder. Apply to face and dust with talcum powder to prevent makeup from smearing.
- To make a beard dab face with vaseline and add coffee grounds. Remove with cold cream.
- If you use commercial makeup on your child, do a "patch" test. Smear a little makeup on a small area of skin on your child's inner arm to check for allergies or sensitivities.

I could have shot the guy. My brave little three-year-old walked up to the house, knocked on the door, and waited politely. It was opened by a gorilla. My son screamed bloody murder and, despite the fact that the home owner took off his head to reveal his human side (which nearly sent my son into convulsions), my little boy would have no more of Halloween that year. Mind you, as a six-year-old he loves to be scared to death.

Parent

- Use self-adhesive toe pads (found in drugstores) to make warts and moles.
- Have your child carry a sand bucket or pail instead of a large bag that may be tripped over. You may want to carry a larger bag and have the child empty the bucket once in a while. If

your child is very young, you may want to say that as soon as the bucket is full it's time to go home.
- Glue reflectors onto loot buckets and costumes. Or toss a turned-on flashlight into the loot bucket.
- Tie a disposable flashlight around your child's belt. Do not loop anything around your child's neck.
- If your children are out on their own give them watches with alarms. Decide what time they are to return and set the alarm.
- Tuck identification into pockets.

Our daughter is diabetic and cannot eat Halloween treats. Instead of banning Halloween we use the barter system. We dump the candy on the table. I give nonedible treats such as erasers, hair clips and little books in exchange for candy. It's not the candy that my daughter likes, you see, it's the treat.

Parent

Safety on the Streets
- To prevent children from eating the booty immediately, feed them a big dinner but limit the liquid. A pee stop "mid-trick" is difficult.
- Always accompany a young child.
- Do not allow your children to crisscross back and forth across the street. Children assume that if they can see a car coming the car can see them. They cannot easily judge the speed and distance of an oncoming car.
- Walk the route with your child in advance.
- No bikes.
- Tell your child that if he gets lost he may go up to a house and ask for help, but he is not to enter the house.

Protecting Your House

Vandalism is often a nasty side effect of Halloween. In many cases children do not realize the consequences of their behavior and while parents must make every effort to educate their trick-or-treaters, home owners should take extra precautions.

- A dark house may signal the end of Halloween to children but might also suggest that the house is unoccupied. Turn off the porch lights but leave other house lights on.
- Remove the pumpkin from the doorway or driveway.
- Normally placid Spot may take exception to doorbell-ringing short people in pointy hats. Banish pets.
- Keep the pathway to the house clear.
- If it can't be nailed down put it away and lock it up. This includes lawn chairs, potted plants, and tools. Lock the garage door as well.
- Sleeves of costumes may dip into candlelit jack-o'-lanterns, so light up yours with a flashlight.

Halloween Party

If you've decided to replace the door-to-door candy gathering Halloween with a home or block party, here are some ideas.

- Cut out cats from black construction paper and draw the details with a white pencil.
- Tape spooky sounds on a recorder.
- Serve pumpkin pie.
- Put pop ("witches' brew") in a black pot. Serve with a ladle.
- Hang up white sheets and shine lights on them to make ghostly shadows.
- Play "Pin-the-Tail-on-the-Black-Cat."
- Call your treasure hunt a "witch hunt."
- Give every party guest a makeup job.
- Make a pinata in the shape of a bat and fill it with candy kisses. (Take an oblong balloon, cover it with several coats of

papier-maché, paint it black, pop the balloon, fill it with treats, add cardboard black wings, and hang up.)

- Use see-through surgical gloves as trick-or-treat loot bags. (Very spooky.)
- Give each child a little pumpkin or a big orange with markers and have him create his own jack-o'-lantern.
- Use other funny veggies to make jack-o'-lanterns. Take the biggest squash, gourd, or zucchini you can find and carve. Add parsley for hair, a carrot for a nose, perhaps green pepper or onion rings could become ears or earrings!
- String pumpkin seeds together to make necklaces.
- Roast pumpkin seeds. Soak seeds first to remove leftover pulp. Spread on a cookie sheet with a few drops of corn oil and salt. Roast at 350°F (180°C) for fifteen minutes or until golden brown.

Christmas

It's not going to happen. The perfect Walton Christmas — when family harmony rings as clear as church bells — is movie hype. It's sad. But if Uncle Harry has partaken a whopping amount of Christmas cheer for the last ten years then don't expect him to turn over a new leaf this year. And your precious angels will not pose cherublike by the hearth. Caught in the "I want" clutches, the best they may be able to manage are whimpers rather than carols. And there are only a handful of marriages that get through the season without the threat of divorce.

Sit down with your spouse before the holidays this year and talk. What traditions do you love? What really bothers you about the way you celebrate? (There is nothing he can do about his mother, so forget that.) Do you resent spending so much time in the kitchen? What can be done about it? Have you both hankered after a Christmas in the tropics but felt too hampered by tradition even to discuss it? Are you afraid that your parents might be lonely? Maybe your parents would like to get away too. The costs and commercialism get us all down — what can be done?

Christmas stress is often caused by:

- Shopping and credit card hangover. Consider opting out of the mega-shopping and doing some charity work with the children. In place of the last-minute shopping, designate a cedar chest (with lock) as your Christmas chest and collect gifts throughout the year. Talk frankly with other adults in your family and ask if they too might be interested in having only the children exchange gifts. Do not take children into a toy store after November 1st and limit the "I wants" by limiting the children's television viewing.
- Extra costs. Discover "free" ways to celebrate; attend carol services, go skating or sliding, participate in your child's school events.
- Driving. Many families drive on Christmas Day. That alone can cause undue stress. Why focus all the attention on one day of the year? How about spreading the family visits over a month?

Every year my mother-in-law, who lives three hundred miles away, complains about our not coming to her house for Christmas. My husband works until nine o'clock on Christmas Eve. But I can't blame my in-laws. Christmas with the grandchildren is a special time.

Last summer we were ready for their annual visit. In July we wrapped gifts, filled stockings, strung lights, cooked shortbread cookies and a turkey, and put ol' Bing on the stereo. It was a Christmas none of us will forget.

Parent

- Having a pre-Christmas party seemed like a good idea back in September but now that December's here. . . ! Hire a teenager to baby-sit while you are entertaining. Better yet, as a Christmas present to yourself, have a baby- sitter come in from nine to five for the days leading up to Christmas. Now you can dash out on errands without having to schlepp your kids around.

Christmas Safety

- Don't leave nuts out in bowls. They can cause a small child to choke.
- Extension cords, especially when run under a rug, can cause fires. Tape them to the wall.
- Avoid using artificial snow on the windows when young children are around. Their little lungs aren't up to it.
- Don't burn wrapping paper in the fireplace.
- Edible tree ornaments mixed with glass decorations confuse children. And placing tempting candy canes way up high will only encourage your toddler to scale the tree.
- Holly, Christmas roses, ivy, Jerusalem cherry, yew, and mistletoe are all poisonous.
- Gently vacuum your home's smoke detectors and check fire extinguishers.
- The home's electrical system will be taxed during the season. Buy a handful of replacement fuses.
- If you are worried about your toddler creating havoc at a relative's home (not to mention putting herself in danger), bring along a playpen.

Traditions

If the old traditions are not working anymore, replace them with new traditions.

There are many definitions of the word "tradition." Sadly the one used most is "repetition." If you really hate baking, don't do it. Buy the shortbread at the school bake sale.

Three years ago I burnt the ham on Christmas Eve. (My family has served a ham every Christmas Eve for four generations.) I was devastated. My husband ran out for pizza. We all gathered around the fireplace and ate it. Two years ago I broke my ankle. We decided to skip the cooking that year and once again my husband went out for pizza. Well this year when I went to buy a ham the kids said, "What, no pizza? How can you break our tradition?"

Parent

The golden rule? Put your family first. That means take it easy. Your child probably prefers to have a cuddle and a favorite story read to her than to live in a home so decorated it looks like a window dressing. It also means take care of yourself. Now is not the time to repaint the kitchen. Like the man says, "Don't worry, be happy."

Here are some traditions to live with:

- Young children have a crummy sense of time. An Advent calendar might help. Or make a chain of twenty-four paper circles and string them up. Your child can remove one circle a day. He will now see that Christmas is getting closer. Or draw a Christmas tree on heavy construction paper. Let your child glue a Christmas sticker or small candy onto the tree every day.
- Give your child a special decoration each year. Store it in a box with her name on it. She alone can then be responsible for hanging these ornaments. And one day they could be the start of her own decorations for her own tree.
- Roast chestnuts. Cut slits in the flat sides of the nuts, toss into a pan of boiling water, and boil for five minutes. Drain. Roast in a hot oven or over a fire for ten to fifteen minutes.

- Use upside-down ice cream cones to make an edible festive centerpiece. Have the kids mix butter with a little milk and lots of confectioner's sugar. Add green or red food coloring. Mix until a paste is formed. Smear on the cones. Decorate with such edible treats as mini-marshmallows and silver balls.
- If it's your habit to throw an adult party every year, why not switch and throw a kid's party in November instead? Invite six or so kids over for a craft party where they can make gifts for their parents.
- *Making Your Own Traditions Around the Year* and *Making Your Own Traditions: Christmas*, by Dette Hunter and Jocelyn Shiply, are available by mail order from Traditions Press, 125 Arden Avenue, Newmarket, Ontario L3Y 4H7.

Decorations

They cost a fortune. What can be done?

- Keep one box or basket handy throughout the year to collect beautiful ornamental treasures picked up here and there.
- Save your child's artwork throughout the year in a convenient place. With your child's permission use the drawings to wrap gifts.
- Wrap boxed gifts in butcher paper and have the children color the wrappings with crayon. (Be careful with paint and markers which may leak through the paper.) Or roll out the butcher paper and have the children paint the paper before wrapping the gift.

  Little ones who are not yet adept at wielding a brush might decorate the packages with finger paints. In a pinch wrap a small gift in a Christmas napkin and add a bow.
- The best thing about stringing popcorn is that you can do it sitting down. Pop the corn the night before and let it sit. Stale popcorn is easier to string.
- If you must spray the windows with fake snow, spray Pam on first. The snow should wipe away easily (but no guarantees).

- Don't throw the tree out. Prop it up in the snow and decorate it with bird food. Watch the birds come and snack.

My three-year-old was convinced that Santa would not make it to our house because we did not have a fireplace. Instead of hanging up stockings we put our boots by the front door.

Parent

Gift Giving

- While stockings planted at the end of the bed may be magical for kids, they also serve to keep them quiet for an extra hour or so on Christmas morning. With that in mind, fill the stocking with gifts for activities — a coloring book and crayons, hand-held games, small puzzles.
- Limit the gift-giving "pig out". Baby Jesus received three gifts, so might your child: a gift she wants, a gift she needs, and a surprise.
- Use stickers or specially colored wrapping paper to differentiate gifts if your children are too young to read.
- Frame a collage of your child's artwork for the grandparents.
- Grandparents might give one gift to a child that will stay in their own home. In that way the toy supply at Granny's house will grow and be shared by all visiting grandchildren.
- Encourage your child to give gift certificates to family members: "This certificate is good for one breakfast in bed" or something of the sort. Your child may get carried away and offer to paint the house. Easy does it.
- Hiding gifts is an art. Here's an idea: — hide your children's presents in old, stored luggage.

Books

Watch the typical reaction of a child when he or she unwraps a book: "Oh yuck, a book." More than likely your child will toss the book into the "oh yuck, clothes" pile. Here are some ways to counter that reaction:

- Make a tradition of giving a child a special book every Christmas Eve. Perhaps you could read a chapter before bed (a great way to calm down an overexcited child).
- Books just don't rank against overpackaged, multicolored, much-sought-after toys. Separate them. Have a book-giving part of Christmas day, perhaps during mid-afternoon (between the Great Gift Pillage and The Great Pig Out).
- How you react to a "book as gift" will set an example to the children. Receive a book with gusto!
- Combine a toy with a book. If, for example, you are giving a young child a book about puppets include a small hand or finger puppet with the book. Plasticine may accompany a book on "things to do with plasticine." A stuffed rabbit might be wrapped up with a book about a bunny. Tickets to a play might go with a book on the theater.

Boxing Day

The post-Christmas blues hit us all but children tend to come off the Christmas high with a particular thud. Break their fall.

- Save one small gift for Boxing Day morning.
- Plan a quiet family activity, a walk in the woods, skating, take in a movie. But if you value your sanity, don't under any circumstances take them shopping.
- If you do take your children on a Boxing Day shopping trip (not recommended), let her pick out a special ornament for next year's tree.
- The days between Christmas and New Year's can be fun if you plan mini- activities, but don't schedule your child's every hour. She'll want to visit her own friends and show off her new toys.
- Drop off a few gifts at a local hospital.
- Take a picture of your child with the gift and send it back to the giver with a thank-you note.

- When no one is looking put away a few of the new toys to save for a rainy day.

Valentine's Day

- Help your child make a simple heart by folding construction paper in half and cutting out half a heart.
- Send cards in code. A-1, B-2, C-3, and so on is a simple code. Or split the alphabet in two; on one side of the page write down the alphabet from A through M and on the other side N through Z. A-N, B-O, C-P and so on. Or teach your kids how a rebus works. The picture of an eye is used instead of "I" The word "you" becomes "U." A picture of a deer is "dear" and so forth.
- Do not send cards to school without inquiring about the classroom policy. Some teachers, fed up with sad, cardless kids, have banned the cards altogether.
- Make heart-shaped cookies. Scrawl names on them in icing and use them instead of cards.
- Give your kids a Valentine's breakfast. Make heart-shaped pancakes or heart- shaped french toast. Serve up strawberry milk shakes. And for lunch — how about a heart-shaped pizza?

Easter

Decorating Eggs

There are two ways to work with eggs. Either blow out the middle or hard boil them. It's best if you give little ones hard-boiled eggs.

- To blow an egg take a needle and pierce both ends. Be sure the needle pierces the yolk. Blow the contents into a bowl. Rinse the outside of the eggshell and let it dry.
- Decorate eggs with nail polish, glitter, makeup, stars, dots. Or glue on cartoon cutouts with egg white. Dribble on wax

from a colored candle. To make stripes, wrap the egg with masking tape. Paint and peel off. Hang the eggs from a tree.

- What's Easter without a new Easter bonnet? A trip to the local Sally Ann will net you all sorts of weird and wonderful hats. Raid Grandma's attic if you can.
- Collect plastic eggs and fill them with treats, poems, jokes, tiny gifts.
- Does the Easter Bunny come to your house? Don't forget to leave a carrot out for him (her?).

9

Birthday Parties

On the way home from yet another snazzy birthday party, complete with magician, clown, and videos, my son asked about his upcoming party. "Are we going to have cake at my party?" he asked. I said yes. "A cake with real cake inside the cake? And will we have real games and normal food?" This bizarre line of questioning went on for some time.

The point soon became obvious. Not all children like the new-fangled, pre-planned, all-encompassing birthday parties complete with rock band, circus, and quiche. Most kids simply want to be king for a few hours, have their friends over, and show off their toys and parents (yes, parents!).

First Birthdays

Some families celebrate two "first" birthdays. Number one may be when baby comes home from the hospital. Traditionally, this party is in honor of the baby but is celebrated by the siblings. If you are planning such a party, buy and freeze a small cake before going into hospital. Keep the party limited to close family and let someone else handle the proceedings. (Chances are all you will want to do is head to bed with baby snug in your arms.)

Turning one is a milestone — for parents. Invite a few friends over, the fewer kids the better. Since this birthday is usually Mom's and Dad's celebration, you might want to hire a baby-sitter to care for baby while you attend to the grown-ups. (Henceforth, birthdays belong to baby.)

My kids send me flowers on their birthday. It's a sweet idea don't you think? After all, I did all the work.

Mom

Children's Birthday Parties

What follows are suggestions for parents who don't care to spend a month's rent money on the party but who want to create a memorable event.

The Countdown

Parties are learning experiences for host and guests. Good manners, self-restraint, social skills are just some of the lessons learned. Involve your child from beginning to end. And remember, the planning can be as much fun as the party itself — which is one reason why surprise parties are not for small children. Start a couple of weeks in advance.

- A rule of thumb: If your child is three invite three children, if child is five invite five, and so on. Hardly anybody sticks to this rule but there would be fewer frazzled parents around if we did.
- Watch the clock. If the child is under four plan for a two-hour party. Extend the length of time by half an hour each year up to a maximum of four hours.
- Talk about past parties, the most and least favorite, and try not to make the same mistakes twice.
- Send written invitations through the mail, deliver them by hand, or make a phone call. Never send invitations through the school unless you intend to invite the entire class! One left-out child might be devastated. Also, invitations distributed at school might not make it home.
- Invitations need not be boring store-bought cards. Cut up old greeting cards, paste them on folded construction paper and send them out. If the invitations are to be delivered by hand paint a small block of wood (perhaps your child's old building blocks) and print the information on the different sides. Or write out the particulars on cardboard and cut up puzzle style. Blow up a balloon, write the info on it with a magic marker, deflate it, and mail.
- Include on the invitations: date, drop-off and pick-up time, place (Jenny's house), address, phone number, map, and RSVP.
- RSVPs: If the guest list is large you'll be deluged with calls, so post the list by the phone and check off each call as it comes in. Or forget the RSVP and simply say, "Regrets Only."
- If you plan to take the children on an outing, say so on the invitation. Remember, each child needs a seat belt, so count the spaces in the cars.
- Many classrooms are now integrated with handicapped and nonhandicapped children. Include *all* your children's friends in the party and if a wheelchair is involved, don't instantly assume that your home cannot accommodate it.

Call up the child's mother and ask her if she can think of ways to make your two-storey home more accommodating. Chances are she can.

- Oops, the party has to be called off because of illness or a family emergency. Now what? Call everyone personally and send "raincheques" — photocopy a personal cheque or make a hand-drawn facsimile complete with raindrops. Write: "Blake's party has been postponed to (date). When you come please present this raincheque."

Excursions

Bowling alleys, children's restaurants, or movie theaters are the traditional party outings for kids but consider too a tour of a newspaper office, conservation area, telephone company, chocolate or cookie factory, radio or television station, or garbage disposal station (a favorite!). Some ballet or theater companies will let you watch a rehearsal. Call and ask.

- Avoid heavily populated places such as circuses, shopping malls, or exhibitions.

My six-year-old was invited to a nine-year-old's birthday party. I dropped him off at the house, had a hurried chat with the mother, arranged for the pick-up time, and left. Later I found out that the children had all been taken to a local circus. The ratio of children to adult was fifteen to one! I was furious.

Parent

- Get rid of family pets during the party. At least one guest will have pet allergies. Then again, a normally gentle dog might get so upset by all the commotion he might take a nip out of a party guest (or vice versa).

- Make sure the ratio of adults to children is suitable, one to four is acceptable for children under six years. Every adult should carry a bag to catch sweaters, hats, and whatever. Be sure that all the children have identification and you agree on the "lost and found" rules. Sunscreen may also be necessary.

Siblings

The birthday kid's brother or sister is allowed to invite one special friend over for the event.

There is five years' difference in age between my two sons. Every year I "hire" my older son to run the games for his little brother's party. Last year I gave him a modest budget to buy special prizes and games. I think he had as much fun as the birthday boy.

Whoever isn't having the party gets to spend a special day with grandma.

My twin girls divide their birthday. In the morning we have a cake for one child and in the afternoon a cake for our other child. They still have a party together but when they ask to have separate parties — we'll be ready.

Parents

Birthday Food

In the scheme of things food is not all that important to kids.Keep it simple. A tray of sandwiches, juice, nibbles, and cake is all you really need.

- Combine Cheerios, Coco Puffs, Shreddies, Capt'n Crunch, and any other breakfast cereal and serve as a nuts and bolts treat.

- Fruit boxes with mini-straws are not for very young children. Blowing out and sucking in can sometimes get mixed up.
- Never use toothpicks in sandwiches or decorations. Use thin pretzels if you need to stab or hold anything together."
- Peanut butter spread on white bread, hotdogs, and grapes can choke giggling three-year-olds.
- Keep a bottle of club soda handy to help remove those inevitable spills from tablecloths and rugs.
- Make birthday ice cubes. Plop one maraschino cherry in each ice cube tray compartment, add water, and freeze. (Recommended for older children only — young children may choke. Also, make sure the children are aware of these ice cube "surprises".)
- Use licorice sticks as straws.
- If the party is in the back yard, make up birthday lunch boxes or bags for each child. Label each one.
- Serve food at different times. The main course (sandwiches, pizza) might be served shortly after the guests arrive and the cake in the middle of the party.
- Doubtless there will be one guest who cannot eat the offerings. If you know about the diet or allergy in advance, ask the little guest's mom to provide a bagged lunch. Spoil the child with such nonedible treats as stickers, crayons, or hair barrettes.
- Serve up mini-rounds of pizza crust (toast may substitute). Offer toppings of cheese squares, pepperoni, green peppers, pineapple chunks, and whatever else moves you. Have the children decorate their own pizza and pop them under a broiler for two minutes.
- Serve pita pockets and let the kids fill them from bowls of munchies (cheese, cooked hamburger meat, meat slices, tomatoes, pickles).
- Spaghetti is always a hit — besides, it makes a lovely mess. Serve up plain noodles (some prefer them sauceless) with different sauces on the side. To continue the theme after the meal put out bowls of uncooked pasta shapes and have the

children make pasta jewelry. (Dye the pasta different colors by dipping it in food coloring.)

- For dessert, line a jello mold with plastic wrap (for easy removal later on). Alternate layers of softened ice cream with crushed cookies. Freeze. Turn the mold upside down on a plate and serve with such toppings as cherries, whipped cream, chocolate sauce, bananas, and Smarties. (Stick a candle in the creation and make it into a birthday "bomb."
- Peel bananas. Wrap them individually in tinfoil and pop in the freezer for one hour.
- Pour 2 cups (500 mL) of juice into a pot and add 2 tablespoons (1 oz, or 30 grams) of gelatin. Mix over low heat for five minutes or until all the gelatin disappears. Pour the mixture into popsicle trays and freeze. To remove, dip the tray in hot water, run a knife around the edges and, wiggle-waggle, jelly sticks!
- Give each child a "personalized" treat. Make giant cookies and scrawl each child's name on them with icing.
- Great homemade cakes have tinfoil-wrapped dimes inside. Place the dimes carefully to ensure that each child gets one.
- Forget the hockey players squaring off on marzipan icing — the best cakes are decorated with smarties!
- If you do not want to use jelly beans or other candies to decorate the cake, use fresh fruit slices. (Canned fruit slices are usually too mushy.)
- Make sure all cake decorations are suitable and edible. Mixing edible decorations with mini-toys is confusing.
- Is your birthday child three years old? Bake a cake in an angel food cake pan. Cut the cake (vertically) in half, flip the top over to form a giant 3! Decorate.
- A cupcake with one candle for each little guest is a nice switch, assuming your child does not object to sharing the flame.
- If the mere mention of baking brings on a migraine buy an undecorated cake and let the kids decorate it.

- Fill flat-bottomed ice cream cones to a little less than the halfway mark with cake batter. Bake. Cool. Add icing. (A great idea for picnic parties.)
- *Punch*: 1 large can of frozen cranberry juice, 2 bottles soda water, 1 cup (250 mL) unsweetened pineapple juice, sugar to taste. Or try 2 large cans of frozen orange or strawberry juice and 2 bottles of soda water; decorate the fizzy orange juice with orange slices or the strawberry juice with fresh strawberries. Or freeze bits of fruit in the ice cubes. (Again, for older children only — and warn them!)
- If your child is between four and seven, gross is great. Here are a few gross ideas. Add a drop of green food coloring to the punch and call it liquid slime. (Look out, they may call it pee.) Drop raisins (squished flies) into the ice cube tray, fill with water and freeze. Sprinkle chocolate slivers on the top of the cake and call it dirt.

Decorations for the Table

- Tie-up crayons or washable markers with a bit of ribbon and place at each table setting. Cover the table with a large sheet of butcher paper. Have the guests draw place mats at each setting while you bring on the food.
- Give each child a place mat (a square of construction paper) and let him color it.
- Decorated toilet paper rolls cut into one-inch lengths make great napkin rings.
- Tuck a surprise or treat into each roll, wrap with tissue paper, and leave at each setting.
- Leave a fortune cookie at each place setting.
- Decorate the room with your child's stuffed pals.
- With your child's permission decorate the room with pictures of past birthday parties.
- Take two balloons, one see-through and a smaller, brightly colored one. Put the smaller balloon inside the clear one. Blow, tie the small balloon. Now pull up the mouth piece of the clear balloon and blow. A balloon in a balloon. Neat!

- Balloons and babies don't mix. Tie balloons way up high so they can be admired but not grabbed by very small children.
- Use a hand-pump for an air mattress to blow up balloons.

Activities

Plan twice as many activities as you think you will need. Here are some ideas.

THE TREASURE HUNT

By far the most successful party activity is the treasure hunt, particularly if you can hold it outdoors. Space, not weather, should be the main concern. Unless there's a typhoon howling outside (and even then), children will battle the elements to get the treasures.

- To discourage ants, wrap edible treasures in tinfoil.
- Hide treasures at different heights.
- Give each child a box or bag, labeled with his name.
- If children range in age, either make up teams (seven-year-olds paired with four-year-olds) or let the young ones have a good head start.
- Once the treasures have been collected, put them on an out-of-reach tray and deliver them to eager hands only when the children leave.
- Keep a handful of treats in the palm of your hand to drop in front of little ones who can't seem to find anything.
- If the children are very small, bury the wrapped treasures in the sandbox. In this case small, plastic toys are preferable to candy. Limit the booty per child or replant treasures to ensure that each child finds at least one toy.
- A variation on the treasure hunt theme (for children who can read): Divide children into groups and hand out a list of collectibles – example, find a white pebble, a red leaf, a yellow flower, and so on. Whichever group finds everything on the list first wins the game.

OTHER ACTIVITIES

It never fails. The party may start at 1:00 but kids keep dribbling in up to an hour later. I always have little activities, such as a coloring contest, planned for this part of the party — otherwise the children just stand in a clump at the door and my daughter frets about who's not going to show up.

Parent

- Hang a sheet on the clothesline and have the children throw frisbees into it. (To make disposable frisbees glue the bottoms of two paper plates together and decorate. Or use margarine tub lids.)
- Instead of Pin-the-Tail-on-the-Donkey, cut a teddy bear out of construction paper. Play Stick-the-Bow-on-the-Bear.

NONCOMPETITIVE GAMES

- Musical Pillows. Instead of eliminating one child and one chair when the music stops, remove a pillow. In the end all the children must "balance" on one pillow.
- Face painting is always popular but use this idea only if you have help. Each face takes time. A thin mustache might suffice for some children while others would like full face makeup.
- Blowing bubbles is a bit of harmless fun. Fill a small bucket with equal parts glycerine and dish detergent (Ivory or Joy are good). String tied in a circle and placed on the end of a stick, wire whisks, straws, and funnels all make good blowers. Experiment.
- Pass-the-Present is an old game that kids still love. Wrap a small gift. Rewrap it and wrap it again and again and again until it is a great big present. Pass it around the circle. Each

child peels off one layer. Whoever gets to the last layer keeps the gift. (Don't be afraid to have silly gifts like a pencil or a rock.)

- Put precooked, cold spaghetti noodles, raw liver, overripe bananas, peeled grapes, semi-hard boiled eggs — and anything else in the fridge that qualifies as disgusting — in a bowl. Thinly coat the entire mess with vegetable oil. Now blindfold your victims and let them dip their hands into this revolting goo and guess what each ingredient is. Delicious fun! (No eating allowed.)
- Another gross guessing game. Put warm beans, stewed prunes, grapes, and anything else you can think of in sandwich-size plastic bags. Blindfold the children. Pass the bags around and have each child guess what is in it. (Not recommended for sensitive parents.)

WIND-DOWN GAMES

- Toss pennies into a bucket. Have the children stand at least four feet away.
- Have the children sit in a circle. Tell jokes. Whoever laughs first must lie down. When all the children are lying down turn down the lights and have a "pretend sleep." Whoever can "sleep" for three minutes (an eternity) gets a prize. (Don't be surprised to find a few party guests catching forty winks.)
- The last game of the day is The-Clean-Up-Game. Dig out your old Snow White record and play "Whistle While You Work." (Any upbeat record will do). Everybody who works gets a prize!

The Big Rip

Watching a child unceremoniously rip open gifts and toss them carelessly aside is not a pretty sight. Party guests get the dubious honor of watching their status rise and fall according to the group cheers. Yuck.

- Think about putting a limit on the cost of gifts.
- While your child opens the gifts give the guests assigned tasks: one child may hold the garbage bag while another stuffs it (later you may have to pillage the garbage bag for boxes or instructions, therefore, make sure the bag has never been used), another child may read out the cards, another may collect the ribbons and bows, and so on.
- If there is an older child present perhaps he could keep a written record of the gifts. Thank-you notes are a must for children over seven years of age.
- Have the guests hide their gifts when they enter your home. Each guest may then give verbal instructions to the birthday child, such as "It's near a plant" or "It's under a picture." Once the present is found the birthday child can open it.
- Inevitably the children want to open blister packs (a feat in itself) and examine individual bits and pieces of each present. The toy is now as good as lost. Decorate a laundry basket. Once the gifts have been opened and reviewed, place them in the basket. Introduce a new game and quietly whisk the basket of gifts away.

As one of the few parents at another child's birthday party, I was almost as embarrassed as the little party guest. He had given the birthday child a popular war hero figure. Apparently the mother of the birthday boy did not approve of such toys. She declared, in front of all the children and us, that the gift would have to go back. The birthday boy wanted to keep the gift and burst out crying. The little boy who gave the gift was so embarrassed he asked to go home. It was awful.

Parent

- To take direct focus off the "gift rip," pass around a tray of snacks or put on some music.

- Unless you specifically tell the parents of the party guests that you do not allow certain toys (guns, for example), be prepared to graciously accept any and all gifts.

Party Favors

"What's in it for me?" asks the guest. Not an unreasonable thought given that she has probably just watched her friend disappear under a mountain of gifts. Enter the loot bag.

- Save money. Use decorated brown paper lunch bags.
- Make a fish pond (a large cardboard box covered in wrapping paper for the pond and sticks with string and paper-clip hooks for the fishing rods will do). Have the children "fish" for their loot bags. (An especially good idea if you opt for giving each child a single small gift instead of a bag of goodies.)
- Avoid really cheap trinkets for the four-and-under set. These toys break easily and may be ingested. Instead, give out small books, measuring tapes, or barrettes. Buy in bulk — a jumbo pack of crayons can be divvied up.
- Gift wrap one item in the loot bag to add to the festive mood.
- Add an apple or other fruit for bulk.
- Gentle comic books are great but fairly expensive. Bookstores that sell end-of-line or out-of-print books may also sell by the pound or in bulk. Stock up.
- If your child's birthday is anywhere near Halloween, you are in luck. Mini-chocolate-bars are perfect!
- Label each bag. That way you will know which guest has not received, or forgotten, her bag.

Theme Parties

- If you have a mud- or sandpile handy, throw a Dinosaur Party. It may be easier to provide small, inexpensive plastic dinosaurs for each child, but if the children are to bring their own, label them with tape and a marker. Serve "bronto-burgers"

- If you choose to have a Dinosaur Party, make a jumbo dino out of construction paper and play Pin-the-Tail-on-the-Dino. Likewise if you are having a Princess Party, play Pin-the-Horn-on-the-Unicorn.
- Place mats might be construction paper cut in keeping with the theme of the party, for example, animal shapes for a Zoo Party.
- Is it winter? How about a Beach Party? In summer throw a Winter Party. (Fill a basket with summer or winter wear and leave it by the entrance. Each child dips into the basket and dons scarf and mittens or sun hat and glasses before joining the party.)
- Call your local fire department and ask about a tour. Have the children meet at the fire station. Parents may wait until the tour is over. When you get home have a Fire Fighter Party. Use a fire fighter's hat to serve snacks, plant a small fire truck on the cake, have a fire fighter race around the garden. Don't forget to ask at the station for free pamphlets, posters, buttons, or coloring books to use as prizes and treats.
- Invite all the children to come dressed as their favorite book character (Peter Pan, Pippi Longstocking, Sleeping Beauty, etc.). As for the gift — a book of course.

When we first thought of having a dress-up theme party, I naturally assumed that the children would come in Little-Bo-Peep-type outfits. Little did I realize that they would come as Bimbo the Blood Sucker and Bosco the Bad. Unless the host makes it plain that scary costumes are out, you might have a few frightened kids on your hands.

Parent

- If you throw a costume party, keep a few spare costumes on hand for the child who comes without one — an old pair of glasses without the glass, a silly hat, scarf and cane will do.

- Other theme costume party ideas: Pets (dress as your favorite pet), cowgirls and cowboys, astronauts, circus, zoo creatures, favorite doll or toy.

THE POOL PARTY

You do not need a giant pool for a splash party — in fact, it's best if you don't have an in-ground pool! Put an inflatable pool in the middle of the lawn. Have the children come in bathing suits. And, assuming that the numbers are small, it's easiest if you supply the towels. (Sorting out which towel belongs to whom is a bore.)

- Hire a teenage "lifeguard" to watch the action.
- Fill balloons up with water and put them in the inflatable pool. It won't be long before the kids toss them at each other.
- Buy a few bags of ice cubes, put the cubes in the pool, and let the kids "cold" foot it around. Cool fun on a hot day.
- Give each child a small plastic boat and have a boat race in the wading pool. (Half-melted ice cubes become icebergs.)
- A second race: Stick a small plastic figure in each boat, attach strings, and see which child can pull the boat to shore without dumping the passenger.
- When it comes time to eat, dump the water out of the pool.

We had our five-year-olds play catch with a dozen Nerf balls soaked in a bucket of water. They were happily drenched within minutes. It was a great success, but a warning. A friend tried to introduce it at a party for rowdy nine-year-old boys. The kids ended up whipping the balls at each other. It's a terrific game, but only if the kids are young and well supervised.

Parent

THE SLUMBER PARTY

Are you mad? Don't even consider it unless your child, and pals, are over eight, and even then expect to have one little unhappy camper demand to be taken home at 3:30 a.m., another wet the bed, and a third sleepwalk. This assumes the guest list extends to no more than three!

- Ask that all the children bring their own sleeping bags but have a few spares handy.
- Be sure to have the phone number of each child's parents. Ask the parents if they are taking the opportunity to have a night on the town. If so, get the number of a grandparent or guardian. In other words, follow all the rules you give to your baby-sitter, for tonight *you* are the baby-sitter!
- Don't even try to tell the kids to go to sleep. At midnight simply turn down the lights and let them sleep where they drop.

THE SCHOOL PARTY

Most schools have birthday traditions. Talk to your child's teacher. If your child's birthday falls during the summer holidays, perhaps you can choose a halfway date during the school year to celebrate it at school.

- On your child's birthday, and with the teacher's permission, send a fruit, cheese, and vegetable platter, complete with dip, to school for recess. Or ram lollipops into an apple and give one out per student.
- Have lunch at day care with your child. Sit on one of those miniature chairs with your child and her school chums.
- Pick your child up at lunchtime and along with one or two choice guests head for the nearest hamburger joint. (Be sure to clear your plans with other parents and teachers.)
- Donate a book to your child's school in your child's name on her birthday.

Thank-you Notes

- A child under seven should not really be expected to send thank-you notes. The exceptions are for gifts that arrive by mail or through a third party. The giver will want to know if the gift was safely received.
- If you do decide to send thank-yous regardless of your child's age, take a snap of child plus gift. Jot down a thanks on the back and post. Simple,effective, and welcome.
- Thank-you notes to faraway grannies might be handmade pictures decorated with kisses.

Manners? All I would expect from a four-year-old is a semblance of civility. After two hours of nonstop excitement even a thank-you will get my applause.

Parent

From Year to Year

- Keep an ongoing scrapbook for your child throughout the year and give it to him on the eve of his birthday. (It's not as hard as you think. Simply reserve a shoe box in a handy drawer and slip in photographs and other mementos throughout the year.) But do not give the book with other birthday gifts. It will be unceremoniously tossed aside.
- Buy one large guest book and, from year to year, have each party guest sign in. Over the years it will become a terrific keepsake.
- Compose a yearly birthday letter praising your child for her latest accomplishments.
- Collect swatches of birthday wrapping paper each year and have your child make a collage in a scrapbook. Include snapshots, cards, and other memorabilia of the Big Day.

- Store all leftover birthday hats, napkins, crackers, and such as you would Christmas decorations. In a few years you can have a nostalgia party.
- Plant a birthday tree with your child. (If you live in an apartment call up your nearest conservation area and ask if they have a tree-planting program.)
- Make a charitable donation in your child's name.
- Arrange for a florist to have flowers sent to your child each birthday. Make it a standing order.
- Start a birthday tradition — throw a birthday breakfast! A candle stuck in the middle of a plate of pancakes has a charm all its own.
- Most children only have the opportunity to have a party on their birthdays. Pity. There are so many holidays to celebrate. How about throwing a kids's party on the Summer Solstice? Arbor Day? *Let's Celebrate*, by Caroline Parry, Kids Can Press, is a Canadian book that explains many unique holidays to be celebrated.

10

Great Occasions and Major Upheavals

Weddings

Should you take your infant to a wedding? Unless you are in the midst of a bout with colic, chances are your newborn will sleep through the whole event. But if you plan to take your two- or three-year-old — go prepared!

- Explain the ceremony to children before you go. A whispered "And now they are exchanging rings," and "now they are going to kiss" may put the ceremony into perspective.
- Bring distractions that will not stain clothes, damage the church, or make noise.

- Bring food — the best distraction known to child.
- Sit by the entrance.
- Let toddler sit on the floor, although crawling under the pews is an activity to be discouraged.

The Flower Girl/Ring Bearer

"Would little Sue like to be my flower girl?" Most parents are delighted to accept. Little Sue may have an opinion of her own, however. Accepting such a role on behalf of a child depends on the personality of both child and bride. After all, no matter how well the ring bearer or flower girl is prepared, he or she may balk at the starting gate. If the bride is nervous and highstrung or likely to declare her wedding "ruined" because of it, it's best to beg off the honor.

If your child is gregarious and loves attention, and if the bride is prepared to handle not only her own jitters but those of a small child, lead on Little Susie!

- If you are buying your child's outfit from a wedding shop, ask if the outfit can be rented or sold back to the store (assuming it's not decorated with grape juice).
- By all means rehearse, but to overdo it might invite fears where there were none before.
- Have a contingency plan. If your child does show signs of wanting to bolt at the last minute, perhaps he or she could walk down the aisle with a bridesmaid. Or parent could stand with the child at the altar before the procession and discreetly sit down when the wedding party arrives.
- Most children will tucker out in the middle of the reception. If you must stay for the whole event, have a babysitter waiting in the wings to whisk away your little angel.
- While as the parent of the flower girl or ring bearer you must be accommodating, you might ask the bride when she plans to have the group photos taken. It's common to have them taken directly after the wedding and before the reception. As

far as you are concerned, the sooner the better. That beautiful outfit has a short life span.

Second Marriages

It's the current trend to involve a child from the first marriage in the ceremony of the second. However, a young child may be ambivalent about the marriage and the pressure to perform might compound these feelings. Although she may not mention these concerns at the time, tread carefully. By all means include her in the plans but watch for stress signals. Give her time to accept the inevitable. Three or four months should do it. Be as realistic as you can. To set the next marriage up as a kind of utopia ("We'll all be so happy together") is to invite disappointment. Remind her of your love and then remind her again and again. And make sure she is happily settled in a loving atmosphere while you are on your wedding trip.

Death and Funerals

Helping Children Understand Death

Death is all around us. It is not possible to protect our children from death, nor should we. Take the opportunities to talk about death as you find them.

Death is not real to young children — at least not the death of the near and dear. And yet children are exposed to death all the time. Dramatic television programs present us all with endless unreal deaths and the evening news gives us edited stories of deaths that fit neatly into time slots. Our highways are littered with dead and dying animals. Despite this, children under seven or so think of death as a temporary thing. Children between eight and nine might acknowledge death but secretly believe that they and family members are somehow exempt from the whole business. But look out for the ten-year-old whose morbid fascination can drive everyone to distraction.

Death is a fact; grief is an emotion. Rather than thinking of grief as mourning for a person, we might view it more as the separation between child and something important in his life. Moving house, changing schools are all little losses that prepare children for bigger losses.

Our old family dog was badly injured and we decided to have her put down. Before the dog died we took our kids to the vet's to say goodbye. Each of our three children had a different reaction. Our three-year-old tweaked the dog's nose and asked if we were going to McDonald's on the way home. Our five year old cried and our eight-year-old simply hugged the dog and whispered something in her ear. A little later I had a small picture of the dog framed and the kids hung it in their playroom. That was their introduction to death.

Parent

- If you want to bring up the topic of death, take your children on a walk through a graveyard and the questions may flow naturally.
- If a family member or friend has died from a disease, your child may want to know the specifics about the disease. In many cases the unstated question is "Will I/you catch the same disease and die too?"
- You may want to give your child something of sentimental value (a book, a favored toy) that belonged to the deceased. Or you may want to ask the child if there is anything in particular he might like to have , given a suitable choice.
- Before you give your child something of sentimental or economic value, ask yourself if you would become angry with him for losing the gift. As only child logic can fathom, your child may decide that the deceased has gotten him in

trouble or that the deceased is mad at him now that he has lost the gift.

- It may be difficult to talk about the deceased. Perhaps you could play one of his or her favorite songs or read from a favorite book.
- If your child insists on the stiff-upper-lip approach to a death, give him an excuse to cry — read a sad book or watch a sad movie together.

My brother had been dead many months before we planted a special tree in his memory. My seven-year-old son dug the hole as best he could and we dedicated the tree to a man we loved. It was only then that my little boy realized that his uncle would not be coming back.

Parent

- Never say that the deceased is "sleeping" — would you go to sleep knowing that you might never wake up? And referring to a death as a "passing" is confusing — children pass grades, bus stops, and wind. And such glib statements as "He's gone to that big restaurant/bar/playground in the sky" or whatever are totally inappropriate. (Having said that, try to be tolerant of others who may say silly things to your child. Most people just don't know what to say to other adults, let alone to small children.)
- The deceased might be an unborn baby brother or sister. Reactions differ greatly from child to child. One child may be secretly glad that she now does not have to share the spotlight and then find herself guilt ridden for having such thoughts. Another child, who really didn't believe that there was a baby in the first place, might just shrug. Be tolerant.

Because we were prepared, to some extent anyway, for my mother's death, we could talk openly with our children, who were four and six years at the time. At different times both children asked questions like "Will Grandma eat hamburgers again?" and made such remarks as "Grandma is mean. She is making everyone sad." Most of the time they were simply accepting of the whole thing.

Parent

- If Grandma dies expect comments like "I hate Grandma." Children who are attempting to voice their confusion should not be censored. Anger, fear, and, in some situations, relief are all part of the survivors' process of coming to terms with death.
- All children express themselves in different ways and at different times. Be tolerant and patient.

Funerals

If your child does attend the funeral service here are some suggestions.

- A child may return from a funeral service and ask to play with his skateboard. Whenever possible, let your child behave as he wishes.
- Should a child view the body? Experts agree that there is no one answer — it depends on the nature and age of the child, the condition of the body, the cause of death, and the family's traditions. A child, however, should never be forced to view, touch, or kiss the deceased. On the whole, most funeral homes are depressing and/or downright spooky and no place for children. Skip the viewing if you possibly can.
- Talk to the funeral director. In some cases, but by no means all, this person may be trained to talk to young children. And,

as a nonfamily member, he or she may be prepared to answer questions like "Exactly what happens to the body?". (Children are not prepared to accept the "dust-to-dust" stuff — they may want specifics like how a body decays.)

- If the funeral service is to be a long one, bring a few distractions such as a coloring book and crayons.
- Unless the death is particularly close (a parent or sibling), most children take their cues from the adults around them. In other words, those tears may be caused by fright (if Daddy is crying, things must be really bad), fear (will I/Mom die?), embarrassment (for a tearful adult), or if everyone is crying, the tears might simply be in sympathy for everyone else.

My son was five when his grandpa died. A family friend asked me if I would like to have some pictures taken of the funeral. I was taken aback at first — snapshots and good times have always been synonymous to me. Taking pictures of the funeral seemed, well, disrespectful. Later I realized that it was a good idea. My son couldn't appreciate what was happening at the time but by reviewing the pictures months later he came to understand and accept the death of his grandpa.

Parent

- No one should buzz around a funeral service popping off flashes. However, pictures taken of the funeral can help a child digest the event at her own pace later on. (They are also welcomed by long-distance relatives who could not attend.) This is a time of stress, however, and some relatives have very distinct views of what is, and what is not, proper. Tread carefully.
- Collect old letters, snapshots, and such and help your child put together a very special mini-album of the deceased.

My daughter wrote her deceased grandma a poem. It was slipped into the coffin. Oddly enough, we all felt a little better.

Parent

Moving House

How a child accepts and adjusts to a move depends on the reason for the move (divorce as opposed to a transfer), who is moving with him and who is being left behind (pet, grandparent), where he is moving to (across the hall or to Brisbane), the stage of his personal development (a two-year- old's perception is different from that of an eight-year-old), and the signals you are giving off (if you are apprehensive your child will be too).

All things being equal, it is fairly easy to move with children under eight. The family is still the center of their world. However, it's important not to minimize children's anxiety. And just as important, do not look upon their friendships as "transferable."

- Help your child say goodbye. Fill out change-of-address forms together and, if possible, deliver them by hand to say a formal goodbye.
- Have a Bon Voyage Party for your child. It need not be a big deal — a few cookies and a bottle of pop. Since you have doubtless helped your child clean out his toy box, you may suggest he give away a few small toys as gifts for his friends to remember him by.
- Take plenty of pictures of your old home, your child with her friends, the old school, the playground, and favorite haunts. You will all want them in years to come, but for the moment your child may use them to have a good cry over — which is

not a bad thing. (Some teachers will be glad to include them in a show-and-tell session in the new school.)

- Tape your child and his friends singing or horsing around.
- Give your child an address book and help her fill in the addresses and phone numbers of all her old friends.
- It would be nice, although it's not always practical, to visit your new home at least once before the big move. If a look-see is impossible, contact the local Chamber of Commerce and ask for street maps and information about the area. If your child is into gymnastics or theater, for example, ask for specifics.
- Before leaving home contact the organizations that your child is a member of, such as Beavers or Brownies, and find out if there are local branches.

We moved often when I was little. My mother was very sensitive to the upheaval. With great hoopla we would plant a tree or bush in the yard of the house before we left. In one country we lived in an apartment. My mom and I hid a small picture of ourselves under the floorboards with a little note of who we were and how much we loved the place. I wonder if it is still there.

Parent

- Make a calendar and mark off the days to the moving date.
- Pack up your child's room last and have those boxes loaded on the truck last.
- It takes patience to scrape that kitten poster off her bedroom wall, but do it anyway. Nothing quite makes a bedroom feel like home as much as a familiar poster.
- Details! Details! "How long will it take to drive/fly to the new house?" "Will you be sleeping in a hotel along the way?"

"The stove is packed — how will we eat?" Explain all these things to your child.

- Perhaps there is a horseshoe hanging over the basement door, a family crest in the living room, a picture of great-great Granny in the hall — every home has some symbol or other. Tuck it into your bag and make a ceremony of hanging it up in the new house as soon as you arrive.

Arrival

- Unpack your child's room first. Make it as familiar as possible.
- Give your child plastic-coated identification to carry with him.
- Be sure to teach him his new phone number. (Assign a musical note to each digit and have him sing it.)
- Get to know the lay of the land. Drive around the block and point out landmarks. Walk around. Walk to your child's school, the store, the park.
- Make a small map of the area and post it on the fridge. (This works with older children; small children do not relate well to maps.)
- Keep to the "if it's Friday it must be hamburgers" routine. Try to maintain as many family habits as possible. This reminds a child that some things, like values and routines, stay the same.
- Make your mark. Plant a bush or tree. Pour a little cement in the corner in the drive and have everyone leave a handprint or thumbprint.
- Don't be in too big a hurry to leave your child with a new slew of baby- sitters. Don't wait too long either.
- Your child will refer to the old place as "home" for quite some time. Chances are he will gradually start to refer to it as "the old place." You know the move is over when your child spontaneously refers to the new house as "home."
- Let your child phone his old friends as often as finances allow. Encourage calls to grandparents as well — any communication that makes him feel connected will help.

- Receiving mail at the new location helps kids settle in. Take out a magazine subscription in your child's name. Encourage grandparents to write.

The New School

- Talk about the new school. Drive past it a few times during the summer. If the playground is open, take a few spins on the swings with your child. Peek into windows.
- In many cases the school secretary is around in the summer. Call and ask for a class list. If you can reach any of the children's parents, ask both parents and children over for an afternoon.
- Get involved in your child's new school: Meet the teacher and principal. After a few weeks arrange to have an interview with the teacher to discuss any problems and new school routines.
- If your child is making new friends fast and you know nothing about them, run the names of the kids by the principal.
- There are ways to encourage new friendships. This whole process is easiest at the beginning of the school year, but don't get too upset if you must move midterm. If you have moved to a small or suburban community, call your child's teacher and ask if there are any children nearby who might buddy-up with your child to and from school. Take your child to the nearest park often. Get him involved in the local clubs or church or synagogue groups. Make your home accessible to new kids, but don't overdo it.
- Parents sometimes inadvertently encourage a child to bribe others into friendship. A parent, for example, might buy an expensive toy or play equipment in hopes of attracting other kids. Don't be tempted. Your child may think that the only way he can make friends is if he has neat stuff, or he may take it upon himself to set the bribes, i.e, start giving away his toys or your money.

11

Travel

Here are some common assumptions traveling families make:

- The children will easily adapt to a new environment.
- They will be entertained by the scenery.
- They will enjoy the new experience.
- They will eat the food provided.

True, some children will positively glory in their new experiences — but the chances of that kid being yours are remote. Be prepared!

Before You Go

- A child's interest in travel plans wanes quickly. Do not involve your child in the plans too early, but don't spring the trip on her either. Sudden trips can discombobulate the most secure child.

- Get a telephone credit card.
- If you must leave a pet behind, explain the temporary pet care Fido will receive. If you don't, your child may assume you are giving the dog away.
- Make sure you are covered by health insurance while you are away from home.
- Contact your child's doctor and ask for referrals to other doctors/hospitals at your destination.
- Bring any necessary medication (in child-resistant containers), copies of regularly used prescriptions, and spare pairs of prescriptioned eyeglasses.
- Bring a first-aid kit (locked in a portable fishing or tool box, which doubles nicely as a step stool in hotel bathrooms).

Safety Note: The medicinal drugs in ASA (aspirin) can be found in any number of medications that go by different names. Because of the possible link to Reye's syndrome, do not give ASA to children or teens. Not all countries are meticulous in their descriptions of the contents of medicines and even if they are, you may not be able to translate.

On Wheels

The democratic method of family discipline was not designed to withstand a trip with three children and a dog. Try a new family motto: The Keeper of the Wallet Calls the Shots.

- Toss a few disposable diapers in the glove compartment. And rather than trying to fit a bulky box of diapers into the trunk, stash them in a pillow cover with a zipper closing and let the kids nap on it.
- Cover the backseat with a large sheet. Cleaning up at the end of each day will amount to a quick shake.
- Stick pictures on the seat facing baby.

- Stash flashlights in the glove compartment along with a small change purse filled with quarters.
- Stash under the seat: a roll of kitchen-sized garbage bags, a roll of paper towels, moist towelettes, a few facecloths.
- Never use a long elastic band to tie toys to a car seat. The elastic might wind around a child's neck.
- The best book to drag along is a department store catalogue (one for each child). Young children will pick out their birthday gifts from here to Mexico. Children old enough to add might be given a budget and told to pretend they are parents with two children and, using the catalogue, they must equip a home with all the necessary appliances, furniture, and extras. Be warned — boys of a certain age will doubtless hover around the ladies' underwear section and drive you batty with giggles.
- Make time for impromptu side trips. One family pulled into a gas station and spotted an arena across the street. They rented skates and went ice skating for an hour. Another family stopped in at a bowling alley.

We were traveling between two Canadian cities on a very, very hot summer day in a car that was not air-conditioned, with two small children and a dog prone to car sickness. We pulled over at a tourist bureau and discovered excellent parks with lakes along the way. We swam in our shorts and T-shirts. The wet clothes went into a plastic bag, we changed into dry clothes, and off we went, refreshed and laughing. It was the best family trip we ever had.

Parent

- Make a book. On the back of most maps you'll find pictures of road signs. Cut them out and put them in a small photograph album (the kind with plastic shields over each page).

Have your child match the signs in the book with the signs on the road; for example, if the first sign in the book is a stop sign, then she cannot turn the page until she sees a stop sign on the road. An alternative is to collect pictures of cars and have your child match the cars in her book with the cars on the road.

- Food is entertainment. Depending on how long the car trip is, you may end up watching your kids turn into blobs! Forget about candies. The last thing you need is kids that are hyper. Sandwiches that lose their filling, juicy fruits, and anything that gets mushy aren't a good idea either.
- Have cooler will travel. It may be tempting to buy a jumbo cooler but if you have a medium-sized car, a small cooler that can be scrunched in the front seat under the passenger's feet is handier — assuming, of course, that the passenger does not now have to dangle her legs out the window.
- Remember, never leave coolers out overnight. Coolers are airtight and can become terrific hiding places for little ones.
- No cooler? No problem. The night before departure pour water or any-juice-but-the-ever-staining-grape juice into a plastic jug. Fill it to the halfway mark and freeze. Top the jug up before leaving. The water or juice will stay cold all day. If wrapped in plastic (to prevent sweating) and placed at the bottom of a watertight bag, it may keep sandwiches cool as well.
- If the last time you tasted powdered milk was in the fifties, try it again. It's not half bad, it's easy to carry, and all you have to do is add water and shake.
- Airtight potato chip cans hold baby bottles perfectly. If baby must have her milk warmed, heat the bottle before you leave, wrap it in tinfoil, and pop it into the tin. It should stay warm for an hour or two.
- Check out the baby-supply section at your favorite baby shop. Look for a straw that fits into the nipple of the bottle. Your baby will now be able to drink from her bottle while in her car seat without anyone having to hold the bottle up in

the air. But be careful: handmade versions of the bottle straw may be dangerous.

What to Bring Along for Infants

- a car seat
- blinds for the backseat passenger windows
- a baby bed for the car (an inflatable baby bathtub is *not* an acceptable substitute — the air-filled surroundings tend to give, and an infant could suffocate if he rolled into the side)
- a rubber-backed sheet to protect the hotel (or Granny's) mattress (but no thin plastic mattress covers allowed!)
- a portable baby bed or small playpen
- a handful of caps for electrical outlets
- an infant carrier or umbrella stroller
- at least two baby bottles with straws
- two small blankets (one to double as a changing pad) and a small pillow
- disposable diapers

What to Bring Along for Toddlers and Older Children

- gentle toys such as stuffed pals or small figures, which give a quiet-time message
- that department store catalogue I mentioned earlier, a frisbee or ball to toss around at pit stops — a terrific way to relieve tension and stretch cramped bodies
- a small shoe bag hung over the backseat passenger window to block out the sun and provide your child with toy storage space
- hand-held computer games (if finances allow)
- one tape deck and headset per child (if finances allow)
- a stopwatch, a pair of binoculars, and a simple combination lock — these will keep children amused for hours

If you are going to the lake or seashore, you will also need:
- sunblock or sunscreen (waterproof)
- hats and sunglasses

- buckets and shovels and balls and frisbees (Put them in a string, mesh or onion bag and dump the bag in the lake to get the sand out before you leave. These bags can also be used to keep drinks cold; put the drinks in the bag and leave them in the lake, weighted down with a rock.)
- umbrella (a large golf umbrella will usually suffice)
- large sheet (to sit on)
- towels for everyone, and two extra
- playpen (the legs will sink into the sand unless you put them in empty cans or jars)
- plastic sandals for each child (thongs slip off in the water)
- jumbo T-shirts
- small first aid kit (if you are at the seashore, you might find it helpful to know that meat tenderizer made into a paste relieves jellyfish stings)
- small radio if you need to hear the weather or traffic report
- hand mirror (to get sand out of your eyes)
- camera
- hairbrush

Remember the days when all you needed was a bikini, sunglasses, and bottle of suntan oil?

Motion Sickness

Nausea, rapid breathing, cold sweat, salivation, and loss of color are symptoms of motion sickness that almost inevitably lead to vomiting. Once motion sickness has started, medication cannot reverse the process. So anticipation and prevention are your best bets in warding off the problem.

- Talk to the doctor before giving a small child an over-the-counter motion sickness drug.
- Put your child on a high-carbohydrate diet for a few days before the trip, but avoid giving her milk or pop just before you leave.

- If you are traveling by car, have the child sit in the front passenger seat and look forward, toward the horizon. If the nausea continues, the child may be more comfortable reclining or lying down across the backseat. Keep a window open.
- Attach a short chain from the rear axle of the car so that it grazes the ground. The idea is to get rid of static electricity. (This idea has been called totally ridiculous by some and extremely effective by others.)
- Do not allow the child to read or color.
- If worse comes to worst, stop the car and give the child her medication and some fresh air. Wait until it has taken effect before starting up. If the child vomits again, do not give her more medication.
- Strong odors, cigarette smoke, heavy meals, reading, and heat will increase the likelihood of motion sickness.
- Sunglasses may help.

In the Air

There are days when one would swear TWC's (Travelers without Children) were never, ever, children themselves — the looks, the hissed comments, the unabashed glares! Even the flight attendants may treat you and your child as plague carriers. Cheer up, you are not alone.

Reservation Checklist

When you make your airplane reservations, ask the agent these questions:

- Do you accept infant seats on board?
- Is a child's menu available?
- How long in advance is pre-boarding?
- Is it possible to book seats in advance?
- What is the bumping policy for families?
- Are "sky-cots" available?

- Are there any special safety rules you should know about? (Canadian Airlines, for example, will not allow children to sleep on the floor.)

Ask if you can fly during low attendance times. Red-eye flights (night flights) may be just the ticket.

When my husband took our three kids (ages two, four, and seven) back to the old country to visit the relatives, the flight attendants treated him like a poor, beleaguered soul or an idiot male who couldn't possibly manage three children by himself. They just couldn't do enough to help him care for the kids. A month ago I took the kids on a three-hour flight and got treated like unclaimed baggage. My travel tip? Let Dad take the kids.

Parent

Boarding

- All airlines offer boarding assistance. Arrive early.
- Some airlines will give an empty seat to a parent carrying an infant while others adamantly refuse. Ask about their policy in advance.
- Dress small children in their sleepers before heading out to the airport. Night attire is conducive to sleep.
- Two-piece jogging suits are the best outfits for older children. (Hopefully a spill will only go halfway.)
- In the United States, technically, any infant seat may be used on an airplane if the seat meets with federal safety standards. The seat can be identified by the sticker saying it meets all requirements. If this sticker has been removed the seat will not be allowed on the plane. In Canada, in most cases, a car seat is allowed on the plane providing the measurements do not exceed those of carry-on luggage. Call and confirm with the airline.

- Do not buckle baby into the belt with you. A sudden jolt forward could crush her.
- If the plan is to rent a car overseas, take your car seat with you. It may be difficult, if not impossible, to rent one when you get to your destination. Pack it up in a box, mark "Fragile" on the outside, and check it in with the rest of your luggage at the airport. A few airlines will provide boxes for your car seat. Again, check in advance.
- Bring an umbrella stroller on board the plane as hand luggage. Hang it up in the suit closet. Finding a luggage cart in the airport is an art.
- Some airlines do provide baby food but it is still a good idea to bring along a small supply of your own. Bib, bowl, spoon, formula, bottle, damp cloth, and garbage bag should all be handy.
- Double diaper baby in the airport. Bring along a quilted or plastic change pad and change baby at your seat. (With any luck the passenger next to you will cooperate.)
- Try not to run out of disposable diapers. However, if you are on the last diaper, pop into the loo and pinch a sanitary napkin. Put it inside the diaper.
- Use the airsick bags for disposing of diapers.
- Always consult your child's doctor before transporting an ill child. If you must travel, bring along a letter of explanation from the doctor.
- Children who suffer from allergies might take along their own pillow and, if there is room, blanket.
- Buckle children into their seat belts before they go to sleep. (Pity the parent that must wake up a two year old because the buckle-up light flashes on.)

Where to Sit

Most parents prefer the bulkhead seats at the front of the plane because there is extra room for a baby's cot. (Ask if sky-cots are available.) The bulkhead seats are also close to the washroom and, if you choose not to have assistance when deplaning, you and family are the first ones off the plane. But there are several disadvantages to the bulkhead seats. The flickering light from the movie screen overhead might bother a sleeping baby,the armrests do not go up, the position of the meal tray makes it difficult to tend to a child during the meal, gear must be stowed overhead (which is inconvenient), and not all planes equip the bulkhead area with oxygen masks. Here are some other things to consider when choosing your seat:

- A child prone to motion sickness is best seated over the wing in an airplane. This is the most stable area in the plane.
- Parents of toddlers tend to prefer aisle seats as they allow them to get up and walk with a toddler. (Never, ever, let a small child walk up and down the aisle alone. Hot coffee may be spilled on her or the plane may hit an air pocket and she may fall.)
- Parents of older children might prefer the window seats during day flying, particulary if the flight is over mountains or, better yet, the Grand Canyon. (Experience says that a younger child looks out a window for three minutes, comments on how small everything looks down there, and then spends the rest of the trip walking back and forth to the washroom.)
- The window seat gives Mom more privacy when nursing, but it's perfectly hellish to climb over two people with a baby in your arms.
- You may prefer to put two children in the seats beside you, which will make it easier to tend to them when the attendants are making their rounds with the food wagons. Or if misbehavior is your worry, have them sit one in front of the other. They can still talk together but punching is difficult.
- If you have a stopover, ask if there are any special amenities for kids. (At Massport's Logan International Airport in Boston, for example, there is a nursery and a play area called Kidport, which provides entertainment, in Terminal C.)

Airsickness

Ear popping and nausea are usually felt during takeoff and landing. Here's how to help your child adjust.

- Give an infant a bottle or pacifier during takeoff and landing. (If the baby is not in a car seat, or otherwise restrained, by all means nurse him.)
- Nasal spray (saline spray for infants) may open clogged nasal passages and reduce the amount of fluid in the ear.
- Play the I-can-yawn-bigger-than-you game.
- Toddlers can suck on lollipops. Older children can chew gum.
- Hold a child's nose closed while he swallows.
- Ask for two moist warm towels to hold over the child's ears. This may reduce some of the pain.
- An oral decongestant may be prescribed by a doctor for children who must fly when they have a cold.
- Children who regularly experience ear and nose complaints may be given prescribed medication. Check with your doctor.
- If the pain lasts for a few days call your doctor.

Hotels

After hours of "Are we there yet?" and "Mommy, Alex hit me," the hotel is a welcome sight. But before the kids take over the room, do a little homemaking of your own.

- Move the furniture in the hotel room to suit yourself. (Unless you specifically tell the chambermaid, she will put everything back in place every day.)
- Put free-standing lights between a chair and a wall and see that electrical cords are out of reach.
- Bring your own set of plug caps. (Unfortunately, North American plug caps will be of no use in Europe.)
- Check the bathroom to see that sample bottles of shampoo, bath oil, and soap are all out of reach and that the toilet lid is

down. Don't forget to remove the complimentary matches from the ashtrays.

- Bring a small fold-up playpen. Most hotel cribs do not meet current safety standards.
- Settle children down quickly. Bring along a child-size sleeping bag.
- Carry a few stickers. Put one under the doorknob of your hotel room. If the kids get locked out and forget the room number, they can look for the little sticker.

Visiting Grandparents or Other Relatives

Maybe it's a family reunion, maybe a trip across the country or across the ocean — but a trip to visit the relatives comes with a multitude of problems (as well as delights, of course). If you are like me, then you too may be tempted to kick off your shoes when you get home and expect Mom to take care of you once more. It's this attitude that puts our children in danger. Stay alert!

- One out of three childhood poisonings take place in the home of a child's grandparents, according to the United States Poison Prevention Council. Homeproof, but be as unintrusive as possible.
- Write Granny a letter or call her ahead of time and suggest that she put away any valuables.
- If you are staying for any length of time and cannot cart a playpen and car seat with you, ask Granny to rent the items. (Planned Parenthood, for example, will rent out infant car seats for a minimal amount. Some baby retail outlets also rent equipment. Check the Yellow Pages and call around. Do not suggest that Granny unearth the crib in the attic. It will not meet current safety standards.)
- Elastic bands strung from cupboard doorknob to cupboard doorknob might ward off your inquisitive toddler.

- Toss a towel over the top of a door if your kids are playing the famous Let's-see-who-can-slam-the-doors-the-hardest game.
- Run a broomstick through cupboard handles.
- Check out the bathroom, particularly behind the toilet (look for toilet cleaner). Put it out of reach.
- Other "hot spots" in Granny's home are: the bedside table (this is probably where she keeps sleeping and heart pills), the kitchen table (near the salt and pepper shakers you may find pills to be taken with meals), purses left in the hall or on the floor.

With all due respect, when it comes to toddler and kid safety, grandparents fall into two categories: those who say "I raised six kids and they all survived" or those who say "I don't want to take my grandchildren for a walk lest they get stolen." Somewhere there is a middle ground and it's up to the visiting parents to find it. If you want grandparents to be comfortable with your kids then you'll have to take the lead.

- Provide grandparents with a stroller that they can push about comfortably. (Tactfully suggest that Granny not put her purse in a front-facing carriage with a toddler, who may open it up and eat the contents.)
- Get your toddler used to a harness and reins before arriving.
- Go with Granny and your toddler on several excursions and talk about the pitfalls.
- Shop for your children's food or bring a few choice items with you. Chances are your young children will not eat Granny's stew, and you will have to deal with Hurt Feelings. Waylay the problem (a little) by preparing the kids' dinners yourself.

Granny's not the only one who has some adjusting to do. Your child may find the experience overwhelming and will need your help to feel comfortable.

- If need be, let your child sleep on the floor of your room for the first night at least.
- Bring along your own night-light and/or give your child a small flashlight for comfort.
- Pack a teddy bear.

My father is a very gruff man. I knew that my four-year-old would be a little frightened of him, so before we left for the cross-country visit we made up some signals. If I touched my nose, that meant "I love you." If I pulled on my ear I was saying, "Isn't this funny?" If I scratched my head I was saying "What a great kid you are." Sure enough, within the hour my father boomed out a command. Instead of crying, my son turned to me, I yanked at my ear, and he smiled. My son soon became used to my father's noisy ways and they became friends.

Parent

- Use snapshots of the relatives to prepare your child for the trip. (Your child might hold a picture of Granny in her hand while talking to her on the telephone.)
- Relatives can often overwhelm a child with hugs and kisses. Some children revel in the attention while others shrink from it. Teach your child to extend her hand if she'd rather shake than hug.
- Your toilet-trained child may quickly become untrained because: she can't find the bathroom, she is too frightened to venture out of her room in the middle of the night or she is overexcited. Bring your own rubber-backed sheets if you have a toddler. In a pinch, place a towel in the target position under the bottom sheet. A plastic bag is not recommended because in rare cases children have bored their way under

the plastic and smothered. If you are going to use one anyway at least put it under the fitted bed sheet.

- Children of any age are susceptible to wetting the bed in a strange place. Keep the hall light on if you can, limit the liquid intake after dinner, and make very sure they go to the bathroom before lights out. Better yet, bring a sleeping bag for your child with a pull-out liner.

It was the funniest thing. Our bathroom at home is at the end of the hall. At our friends' house the kitchen is at the end of the hall. We were playing cards around the kitchen table when our seven-year-old came padding down the hall. He took the lid off a small garbage can, peed, put the lid back on, and trekked on back to bed.

Parent

Lost!

- Carry a recent, unsmiling picture of your child with particulars listed on the back. If you and your child become separated in an airport, for example, hand the picture and description over to the authorities. If you are traveling overseas the child's passport will suffice, providing it is brand new.
- Dress children in look-alike bright clothes. They will be easy to spot from a distance. (However, don't even think about trying to dress a ten- year-old-boy up like his five-year-old sister. It will not work.)
- Put a harness on little ones. They can stretch their legs, work off lots of energy, and not wander off. (If using a harness is not your cup of tea, consider buying a wrist-to-wrist lead. They may be found in child specialty stores or made with a

length of coiled telephone-type cord, two material swatches, and a piece of velcro.)
- Decide on the tactic the family is to take if separated. Young children may be told to ask a mom or grandma with children for help, a uniformed person, or a shopkeeper. Older children may be taught to go to a predesignated spot and wait.
- All children, regardless of age, should carry identification. Using a diaper safety pin, secure the information to the inside of a child's clothing. On the back of Mom's or Dad's business card list emergency numbers at the points of departure and arrival. Make a note of any emergency medical information (diabetes, allergy to medication, etc.).
- Teach children how to operate pay phones in a foreign country and make sure they know enough about the currency to manage this.

Overseas Travel

Things to Take
- a heating coil, found in U.S. camping stores (they are illegal in Canada)
- boxed, nonrefrigerated milk
- water purification tablets
- diapers
- soap, washcloth, and toilet paper (and, if necessary, Johnny seat covers or a portable potty)
- first-aid kit
- car seat and sleeping cot (if applicable)
- battery-powered smoke detector
- sunscreen and sunglasses
- dried chicken noodle soup mix or some other favorite instant food that will be familiar to your child when all else is strange
- extra infant formula (Mead Johnson, Wyeth Labs, and Ross Laboratories all distribute their products overseas. If you have problems getting infant food products, call the American embassy once in the country and ask if you can shop at a base store.)

- Swiss army knife and/or can opener
- a weight lifter to carry all this stuff

Passports

- It is best that each child have his own passport, visas, and permits in case he must travel alone in an emergency. Once a passport is given to a child, repeat documents will not be issued.
- If you are divorced or separated, make very sure that all custody papers are in order before leaving the country.

Home Away from Home

I bought my three-year-old a whole new set of clothes for the trip. What a mistake. He hated them. Part of the problem was that he was already disoriented. The new clothes just compounded the problem.

Parent

- Bring along several small toys. Other children in the airport, on the plane, or wherever will be attracted to the toys and, presto, an instant friendship will bloom. Be prepared to lose the toys. Carry spares.
- Before you leave, obtain a list of English-speaking doctors from The International Association for Medical Assistance to Travelers, 736 Center Street, Lewiston, NY, 14092, U.S.A. This list is free and will come with several handy-dandy information sheets. Lists are also available from Intermedic, 777 Third Avenue, New York, NY, 10017, U.S.A. A membership fee is required before obtaining their list.
- Find out if and where the nearest consulate is in the visited city.

- American citizens might make use of the Citizens' Emergency Center, which provides information on more than fifty foreign countries. This organization also assists Americans who run into trouble overseas. Call 1-202-647-5225. To learn about visa requirements and immunizations write to the U.S. Government Printing Office, Washington, DC, 20402, U.S.A., or call the Publications Request Line at 1-202-783-3238 and ask for Publication No. 9517.

Film Tips

Children's experiences quickly become jumbled. Snapshots help them remember and categorize. Protect your film!

- Some old X-ray machines cause film damage. Put all your film in a small, clear, plastic bag and keep it handy. Have it inspected by hand.
- Buy all the film you will need at home and bring it with you. Chances are it will be fresher and reasonably priced. (One parent spent $22.00 Canadian on a roll of twenty-four in Zimbabwe.) You can, however, get good deals in places like Hong Kong. Talk to your travel agent.
- Don't store film in the glove compartment or trunk of your car.
- Bring along a simple one-step camera. Your child will want to collect her own memories.
- To discourage thieves use an old, tattered camera bag with zip locks.

Parents Traveling without Kids

Most children will resent being left behind, no matter how well parents explain themselves. If you call home and they won't talk to you, be understanding. It's their way of telling you that they are angry.

- Make a calendar. Mark off your day of departure and the day of return. Your child will cross off those days in between. Or make a special calendar with doors (like an Advent calendar) for the days you are away. Leave a message behind each door. Day 1: "Check under your pillow for a special message." Day 2: "Check the silver package on the second shelf in the fridge for a special treat." Day 3: "Watch for the mailman today." Day 4: "Call Aunt Heidi and wish her happy birthday," and so forth.

- On a hectic business trip it's often difficult to pop into a toy store and get exactly what you're looking for. Buy a return gift for your child before you leave and hide it. Now all you'll have to do is pick up a T-shirt at the airport.
- Mail a postcard a day to your child, starting a few days before you leave. The postcards will then start arriving the day after you leave.
- Post a map and mark off your various destinations. With stickers in hand, your child can mark off your stops.
- Freeze a favorite dinner that you cooked to be eaten when you're gone. The familiar taste will be a comfort.
- Tape a few stories to be played back at bedtime.

Of course, you may want to take your kids with you on a business trip. Some hotels (the Hyatt chain, for example) go out of their way to accommodate business people who choose to bring their children along. Contact a travel agent, explain your plans, and ask for family accommodations or any special deals or programs offered in your destination city. No luck? Try another travel agent or call the local Chamber of Commerce in your destination city.

Kids Traveling without Parents

Mom lives in Phoenix and Dad lives in Regina. The lone traveler commutes between. If she is to travel on her own safely, she will need a little help.

By Plane

In some cases children as young as five are allowed to travel on a plane by themselves, providing the flight does not involve a connection. (Check, some airlines do not accept children until age seven.) It is scary to be so little and traveling all by oneself. The first thing a parent must do is try to make a child comfortable with the idea. Include the child in all of the travel arrangements if you can. The idea is to encourage a little travel savvy.

RESERVATIONS AND CHECK-IN

- Try to make a reservation on a flight without any connections.
- Inform the ticket agent that your child will be traveling unaccompanied.
- Take care of all the details yourself. Do not leave it up to the airlines.
- Unaccompanied minors (UM's) under the age of eighteen traveling from Canada to the United States must carry a letter from their parent or guardian stating the purpose of the visit. This letter should also contain the names and addresses of the people the child is to stay with. It should be notarized.
- At check-in (if not before), you will be asked to fill out a form stating where you may be contacted in case of emergency and the name of the individual who will be picking up the child. (Identification will be required from the person meeting the child.)
- Ask about children's meals.
- Is there a movie on the flight? If so, you will want to see that the chosen seat has a good view.
- Make sure the child is well away from the smoking section. In some cases the child may be seated with or very near a traveling family or close to the flight attendants' work station.
- Send the person meeting the child at the other end a photocopy of the ticket. Contact him/her by phone to confirm the time, flight number, and airport. (Some cities have more than one airport or more than one terminal in the airport.)

- Write out the travel plan, from beginning to end, and give two copies to the child. One is for her coat pocket (to refer to) and the second is buried deep inside her belongings, just in case.
- Do not leave the airport until the plane your child is on has actually left the ground.
- When the plane has left the ground, call the person meeting the child and let him/her know whether the plane is on time or late.
- Arrange a backup, just in case the person meeting your child has a flat tire or some other emergency.

ON BOARD

- Have your child dressed in a comfortable jogging suit for the flight.
- Tell your child to ask for a pillow and blanket as soon as he gets on board.
- Give your child enough pocket money to pay for incidentals on the flight. (There is often a charge for stereo headsets and such.)
- Do not forget to give her an identification pack with her name, airline, flight number, destination, lots of phone numbers, and medical notes.
- Off-duty flight attendants may be traveling on the flight. Ask. Your child may be able to sit with them.

LUGGAGE AND PACKING

- Too much luggage can cause problems. One suitcase and one backpack is enough to worry about. (If the trip is extended, a trunk may be shipped separately, leaving the child to bring only her knapsack.)
- Explain to the child how the luggage stubs match the tags on the luggage.
- It is tempting to send only brand-new clothes but remember, those old comfy clothes may make her feel more at home.

Toss in a favorite pair of pajamas or an old sweater, even if they do have holes in the elbows.

- Don't be surprised if your child wants to take an old toy that she has long given up. Unless that old toy of hers is a six-foot bear, go along with it.

CARRY-ON PACKS

- A backpack is easy to manage and it leaves the child's arms free. The pack might contain: a few edible treats, an activity book, crayons, children's books or magazines, a small toy, a tape deck and headset (radios are not allowed on planes), and gum to chew or a lollipop to suck on while taking off and landing. Add a surprise note from you telling him how brave he is. A tiny wrapped present might be nice too.
- Make some room for a quick change of clothes or, at the very least, an extra shirt and sweater. A pair of socks to wear during the flight is a nice idea as well. Add a brush, comb, and toothbrush and paste, and he is all set.

CONTINGENCY PLANS

- Ask the airlines about the policy for delayed or missed flights. What would happen, for example, if an airport closed down and the plane was forced to go to another city? Who would be responsible for the child and where would she stay overnight? (The airline will accept full responsibility, but naturally you will want details.)
- Encourage your child to ask questions like: "What would you do if you could not get to the airport in time to pick me up?" In this way a child may begin to understand the meaning of contingency plans and how to deal with unexpected situations.
- Discuss your views on talking to strangers. For example, what would your child do if she were sitting beside a very nice lady on a long flight who offered to play cards with her? Dealing with strangers is exactly the sort of thing she will face when traveling alone.

- A good supply of quarters is a must. Does she know how to operate a pay phone, use long-distance area codes, and call collect?

By Train

Children over the age of eight are allowed to travel unaccompanied on trains under specific conditions. Amtrak, for example, will allow children in this age group to travel as UM's as long as travel time is during daylight hours. Forms will have to be filled out at the station and the station manager may request a brief interview with the child. Children who travel by themselves will pay full fare.

- Request a pass from the station manager to accompany the child right onto the train. Look around for a traveling family and introduce yourself and child. The idea is not to give a traveling mom or dad yet one more responsibility, but in my experience moms and dads are very protective of other kids on their own.
- If you prefer that your child not talk to anyone during the trip, seat her near the washroom. Make sure she knows how to work the washroom lock.
- Luggage on a train is a real problem. Keep it to a minimum and be sure that all of the child's necessities for the trip are in her backpack and not in her suitcase. Chances are the case will be stowed up high and she will not be able to reach it.
- Tip the conductor well. (You might even ask the conductor to take your child up to meet the engineer sometime during the trip.)

By Bus

Do not send a young child on a long bus ride alone. Buses do not have attendants, and placing the responsibility of caring for a small child on a bus driver is neither fair nor safe.

Arrival

Sometimes children worry about their reception. Will Daddy's new wife like me? Will Grandpa and Grandma remember me? Will Mommy be waiting for me? It might help if your child picks out a special gift for her hosts. This small offering might break the ice.

Traveling alone can be a big adventure for your child if she is prepared for the trip and encouraged to enjoy herself. Don't scare her with endless lists of what not to do; trust her to follow the rules you've always taught her at home and concentrate on helping her look forward to her moment of independence.

12

Kids on Their Own

Latchkey Kids

It's a problem. And a worry. Before you even consider leaving your child to his own devices before and after school, do some reading and check the options.

Fearful of telling others that their child is alone, many families are unaware of the community services that are available. After-school or library programs are growing by leaps and bounds. Day care may offer programs for latchkey kids. Stay-at-home moms may welcome a child for a few hours.

After-school activities such as band practice, theater rehearsal, and basketball may cut down on afternoons spent alone. Is there a sports club or recreation center near your child's school that offers tennis or swim lessons? If so, rent a locker and have your child keep all her equipment at the club.

Jessie, an enterprising ten-year-old, accompanied his teacher home once a week. For a price he raked the lawn or shoveled the snow, walked the dog, took out the garbage, and occasionally vacuumed and dusted. It wasn't long before his services were in high demand by other teachers! Terry, an eight-year-old, entertained a neighbor's four-year-old while the child's mom made dinner.

Sometimes there are no options. Concentrate then on making the experience as positive as possible. Some of the following suggestions will be inappropriate for your circumstances, others will work well. Check them out and decide accordingly.

Remember, your attitude will color your child's experience. If you bombard a child with a list of "don'ts" and suggest that disaster is a thoughtless act away, then fear may be the dominating emotion. This can be a positive experience. Boost your child's confidence.

Getting Up and Out

- If you have to leave for work before your child leaves for school, set an alarm. When it goes off it's time for him to leave.
- Is there an older child in the neighborhood who might pick your child up on the way to school? Call your school and ask. (I don't want to sound sexist, but parents who have used this idea say that it's best if the "escort" is a responsible teenage girl, preferably one who has had some baby-sitting experience. Pay her by the week.)
- Doors that lock automatically can be a real pain, but, expecting a child to remember to lock up may be inviting trouble.
- Every parent likes the idea of serving a hot breakfast. One of the easiest appliances to operate is the microwave. As soon as you think he is able, teach your child how to heat a breakfast in it.

- Another appliance that needs a minimal amount of supervision is the toaster. Look around the dairy case for pop-up meals. It goes without saying that children must be taught not to poke anything in a toaster.
- Stoves are dangerous. It's best if this appliance is ignored altogether.

Home Again

- Leave food out for your child to snack on when she gets home. Certain foods are more comforting than others. Cereal, homemade cookies, and milk, for example, are all traditional foods that are welcoming.
- Welcome a child home from school with warm, not hot, chocolate by filling a thermos in the morning and letting it stand on the counter. Or load your automatic coffee maker with instant hot chocolate and set the timer. The second idea works best if you have a coffee maker that doesn't keep the liquid too hot. Scalds and the potential for breaking a glass pot are two things to keep in mind.
- Use timers anywhere and everywhere. In winter set the lights to come on before your child enters the house.
- Listen to the sounds of the house with your child. Windows rattle, branches may graze the roof, furnaces and fridges come on and go off, pipes gurgle, and foundations creak.
- Get a pet. Dogs are preferred but even a bird or hamster is better than nothing. (If allergies are a problem, why not get an ant farm or put a bird feeder on the windowsill?)
- A taped message or a note stuck on the fridge is reassuring.
- Phone home at preset times.

THINGS TO DO AFTER SCHOOL

- Your child may begin such dinner preparations as setting the table, mixing things, or setting out ingredients. (Carrie, age nine, makes a fantastic Caesar salad dressing.) Cooking and wielding knives, however, are not recommended.

- A few chores can be time consuming and reassuring. However, these chores should have been mastered by the child a long time ago. If a child has not regularly loaded the washer, now is not the time to learn.
- If you are paying your child for certain chores, make a written contract.
- Puzzles, crosswords and coloring are all quiet activities that could be left out for your child to do.

PROBLEMS

- A flashlight and small first-aid kit must be handy.
- Children need friends. Since you can't have kids in your house when you are not there, perhaps your child could visit other homes after school and ask friends over on the weekends.
- If there are other siblings who are also latchkey kids, write down the consequences of inappropriate behavior and post them. That way no one child is responsible for laying down the law and all will know what's expected.
- Avoid handing out rules that are not enforceable. Telling kids not to talk on the phone is not an enforceable rule. Children often use the television and the phone as company. Think carefully before banning them.
- Ask your child to tape his piano/music practice.
- If possible, program the main phone with preset emergency numbers, including the neighbors, your office, police, ambulance, fire, taxi, Grandma, poison control and hospital.
- Post written instructions that would direct an emergency vehicle (an ambulance, for example) to your home. (Children may know their address but may not know surrounding cross streets.)
- Leave an emergency envelope in an accessible drawer containing telephone numbers, health insurance and hospital card, doctor's name and number, and a small amount of cash.
- All children have fears. Find out what your child's are and talk with her about them.

- There are all sorts of telephone lines, such as homework help lines, that are free of charge. There are even phone numbers to call that will recite a story or two. Call your local library and find out which ones are appropriate and free.

LATCHKEY KID SERVICES
It would be difficult to list all the services across North America but as an example in Toronto you can call Kids Connection (416) 698-0304. Kids Help Line is a national, toll-free line. Call 1-800-668-6868.

Money Management

It doesn't take children long to figure that out that money really does make our world go around. Hence, The Allowance!

Most experts do not recommend tying household chores or behavior to the allowance. An allowance tells a child that she is important, that she is responsible and that she is a valued family member. Her value should not go up or down because of her grades or the state of her room. Rather, the idea of an allowance is to teach children how to live on a specific sum of money.

Some people feel that a child should not be given an allowance. They feel that they (parents) should provide for all the child's needs. The result? In some cases the children of these parents learn to manipulate them for money — a smile for a dollar, a bed made for a quarter.

Dishing Out the Bucks

- If there are strings attached, state them in advance. A specific weekly sum might, for example, be set aside for books or charity.
- Dole out the allowance on the same day each week.
- My son loses everything. I keep his allowance for him until we get to the store," is a common statement. Give the child

the money. Part of money management is learning to keep it safe.

- Without turning into a dogmatic Scrooge, do not let kids borrow ahead.
- Once or twice a year review the amount of the allowance, perhaps at the start of the school year and at March break.
- If the allowance consistently runs out midweek, review the situation with your child. She may not be budgeting properly, in which case help rather than criticism is in order. However, it may be that the allowance is too small.
- If your older child wants extra money let him earn it. Chores that do not need to be done every day, like cleaning out the attic, might be jobs that you could pay for. Post a list of kid-size jobs on the fridge along with their monetary worth.
- It may annoy you, but let your child buy junk. Value for the money is easier learned while young.
- Open a bank account for your child and make her responsible for the bankbook.
- Let your child choose specific grocery items on a limited budget. For example, "We have $10.00 in our budget for junk food (popsicles, pop, chips). You decide what we should or should not buy."
- Point out the differences in prices on similar food items while shopping. Talk about quality, price, and quantity.
- Try not to be too nosy about where the money goes, but don't abdicate responsibility completely. If your child is taking money to school, for example, and mysteriously losing it, there may be a bully in the wings. On the other hand, your child may simply be buying chips and pop.
- Children and parents may contribute to a family piggy bank. When the nickels and dimes add up to a specific amount, everyone can go out to a movie. (Alas, there may not be enough money in the kitty for jumbo boxes of popcorn. Try not to reach into your own pocket to make up the difference. There is a lesson to be learned here.)

- Let your children in on the family budgeting. Show them how you keep the family books. More important, show your children a credit card bill and let them see you pay it. Most children believe that owning a credit card is a license to spend. Likewise, the bank machine will need a great deal of explanation.
- Saving and hoarding are two different concepts entirely. A portion of your child's allowance should go to savings, perhaps for something specific. However, spending a little isn't all that bad either. The idea is to encourage balance and moderation.
- You might buy your older child a few shares of stock and teach her how to follow it in the newspaper. If this idea is not appropriate, then pretend to buy stocks with play money. (A trip to the Stock Exchange might be fun too.)

General References for Parents

Michele Lansberg's Guide to Children's Books, Penguin, 1985.
Painless Parties for Young Children and Their Parents, by Shelley Tanaka, Douglas & McIntyre, 1988.
The Canadian Parents' Sourcebook, by Ellen Roseman & Colleen Darragh, Doubleday, 1986.
The Mother's Almanac, by Marguerite Kelly and Elia Parsons, Doubleday, 1975.
The Mother's Almanac II: Your Child from Six to Twelve, by Marguerite Kelly, Doubleday, 1989.
The Childwise Catalogue: A Consumer Guide to Buying the Safest and Best Products for Your Children, Pocket Books, 1986.
No-Fault Parenting, by Helen Neville and Mona Halaby, The Body Press, 1984.
Special Times for Parents & Kids Together, by Lisa Lyons Durkin, Warner Books, 1987.
The Mommy Manager, by Paula Linden and Susan Gross, Franklin Watts, 1987.
Parent Tricks-of-the-Trade, by Kathleen Touw, Gryphon House, 1987.
Practical Parenting Tips, by Vicki Lansky, Meadowbrook, 1980.
Baby Hints, by Chris Casson Madden, Fawcett Columbine Books, 1982.
Making Your Own Traditions around the Year and *Making Your Own Traditions — Christmas*, by Dette Hunter and

Jocelyn Shipley, are available for $9.95 plus $1.00 postage by writing: Traditions Press, 125 Arden Avenue, Newmarket, Ontario L3Y 4H7. Phone: (416) 895-2420.

There are hundreds of different bookstores that will provide phone or mail service to individuals who do not have access to good bookstores. The following are examples:

Parentbooks, 201 Harbord Street. Toronto, Ontario M5S 1H6.
Phone: (416) 537-8334.

Children's Book Store, 604 Markham St., Toronto, Ontario M6G 2L8.
Phone: (416) 535-7011.

Britnell's Book Shop, 765 Yonge Street, Toronto, Ontario M4W 2G6.
Phone: (416) 924-3321 or 1-800-387-1417.

Cardinal Books offers selected books for different ages and reading skill levels. P.O. Box 64, Station S, Toronto, Ontario M5M 4L6.
Phone: (416) 482-5145.

Index